FIRST STEPS IN RITUAL

Frontispiece: The Image of the King
(Jo Gill, from the *Servants of the Light Tarot*)

FIRST STEPS IN RITUAL

Magical Techniques for Experiencing the Inner Worlds

DOLORES ASHCROFT-NOWICKI

Illustrations by Wolfe van Brussel

THE AQUARIAN PRESS

First published 1982
This revised and enlarged edition 1990

British Library Cataloguing in Publication Data

Ashcroft-Nowicki, Dolores
First steps in ritual: magical techniques for
experiencing the inner worlds. — 2nd rev. and expanded ed.
1. Magic. Rituals
I. Title
133.4'3

ISBN 0-85030-874-7

*The Aquarian Press is part of the Thorsons Publishing Group,
Wellingborough, Northamptonshire, NN8 2RQ, England*

Typeset by Harper Phototypesetters Limited, Northampton, England
Printed in Great Britain by Mackays of Chatham, Kent

3 5 7 9 10 8 6 4 2

FOREWORD

In recent years a number of books have given the principles of magical ritual. This is an advance, in my view, on those books that simply reprint rituals, often garbled or incomplete, of individuals and organizations of the past. There may be an historical purpose served but for the most part such material is either too advanced or too idiosyncratic to be of practical use to the inexperienced.

Dolores Ashcroft-Nowicki's book gives another dimension to previous books in that she gives a number of imaginative and practical approaches to the subject, together with explicit elementary instructions for the absolute beginner.

As a result, I hope that much of the portentous obscurity and sinister glamour may be stripped from the subject. Ritual can be a rewarding means of self-expression, self-discovery and exploration of inner realities behind material existence. It is, at the same time, a system of psychotherapy and a creative art. Like its sister disciplines, much will depend upon application and natural talent. In skilled and dedicated hands its potential is enormous.

GARETH KNIGHT

To
Mike, Tammy and Carl,
and to
Basil,
who made me sit down and write it.
Thank you.

CONTENTS

PREFACE TO REVISED EDITION

In the seven years since this book was first published I have learned a lot more about many things, about magic, about ritual, about writing, and about myself. This is the way of magic — you never cease to learn and to improve on what you learn. Because of this I have welcomed the opportunity to enlarge and revise the contents of the book. I have had many letters from readers over the years, all of which have been very gratefully received and read, and to a great extent the contents of such letters are the basis of this new edition. By listening to people who have read and used the book, and by taking note of their experiences and findings, it has been possible to improve and add to the contents in a way I sincerely hope will make it useful to a whole new readership.

I have learned that there are a great many solo magicians out there. Some prefer to work alone, finding it easier to concentrate their mind and powers on the task to hand. Others work alone because there is, as yet, no suitable partner or group available to them. In contrast to this state of affairs, in the past seven years I have been able to bring together large numbers of people, anywhere between 25 and 70, to work ritual magic during weekend seminars. These have been utterly magical in every sense of the word and have brought together people of many different traditions to work in harmony, something that in the old days would have been impossible.

To those who prefer to work alone let me say this; you follow an ancient path. It is a valid and ultimately rewarding path and, for those who work alone because of circumstances, remember that all magic is a means of undergoing tests of character and discipline; it may be that your seeming isolation is part of such a test. For you I have included solo rituals among those added to this new edition. There are also new rituals for those who work within a group situation.

I have deleted some of the rituals in the previous edition because my mail bag indicated that they were mostly left unused or they did not find a place within the work schedule of Western magic. The most popular of all were the Egyptian, the Orphic, and the top place went to the Celtic ritual which caught the imagination and hearts of everyone. I have heard of it being done in the ripening cornfields of Mid-West America, on Welsh mountain tops, in English meadows, and inside stone cricles — even on a deserted beach in Greece. I hope that the new rituals included here will give as much to heart, mind and spirit as did the old ones.

I am always interested in hearing from readers who have worked the rituals and would like to share their experiences with me. After all, who knows, I may be able to improve on this edition.

DOLORES ASHCROFT-NOWICKI

1. INTRODUCTION TO RITUAL

There is no quick and easy way to learn the art of ritual, no short cut that will eliminate hard work, dedication, and a great deal of self-discipline. There is only one way: start with something simple and learn your craft by trial and error. This is true even if you are lucky enough to join a group or a school willing to teach you. By doing this, you will lay down a foundation of experience that will serve you well in future work.

In all the many years that I have been teaching occult science, ritual without a doubt continues to be the most over-emphasized and, at the same time, the most misused part of that science. The main trouble stems from the fact that most would-be magicians think that the reading of a few books, attendance at one or two seminars, a robe and some incense are all that they need to become an adept. They could not be more wrong. It amounts to setting up as a surgeon having read one's way through a home medical encyclopaedia: in most cases it is every bit as dangerous. I have had more years' experience in dealing with ritual than I care to remember, but there are still some that I would think very carefully about before I attempted them. Come to that, there are some I would not consider at any price, simply because I am aware of the risks involved.

It has been claimed that all magic is evil, and that its practice 'can send you mad'. The first statement is untrue, but the second is quite true: it can. So can alcohol, drugs, and inherited mental flaws, to say nothing of the pressures of modern living. But it is not evil in itself. Only the purpose to which it is put, and the personality of the individual using it, can be evil. It is not always fully realized that ritual places enormous pressures on those who perform it, both on the mental and spiritual levels, as well as on the physical. It is important, for instance, to keep fairly fit. The idea of the obese, drug-soaked and over-sexed magician, so beloved of the lower echelon of occult writers and reporters, is a non-starter. Such practices would seriously inhibit any truly magical work from the humblest spell upwards . . . or downwards, whichever way one looks at these things.

Blood pressure can rise considerably during some rituals, so you must be prepared to go slowly and work up to the performance of bigger rituals. The most important thing is to undergo some serious training, and learn to balance the forces within yourself. Any occult school of repute will tell you that before any ritual work can be done, the personality must be tested and its weak points found and strengthened. Without this, you can come to grief in any number of ways, none of them particularly pleasant. If there is a mental or personality flaw anywhere in your make-up, be sure that ritual will find it out and put pressure on it until you break. It is this that can undo the hopeful magician, not the work itself. It may seem tedious, and at times even boring, to go through the first years of your occult training doing nothing much in the way of ritual, but those years are vitally important. Learning to know just where to expect a weak spot in yourself can save a lot of trouble later. In fact, 'knowing yourself' is the first and one of the most important steps in ritual. However, for those who, though with some way still to go in their training, would like to do some basic ritual work, a book of carefully constructed rites aimed at gently stretching their newly budding abilities seems to be the answer. After seeing some of the things students have attempted in the past, I came to the conclusion that it would be better to provide some work of the sort that even a comparative newcomer could perform without coming to grief.

Full-scale rituals need a fully trained group of officers, and a consecrated Temple in which to work; add to this, equipment, robes, nerve, and a lot of know-how. However, all the rituals in this book are designed to bring about a reasonable amount of effect, even if performed with a minimum of experience. Having said that, I should point out that as you grow in ability, so will the effect of the rituals. You will, in fact, grow together. The rituals are arranged to provide for one, two, four, or a group of people. As with the first edition of this book, I have placed them in categories of traditions. It is important for a would-be magician to get used to working with a variety of different god-forms and traditions. Out of this will come a preference or talent for one or two in particular, which can then be extended into a full-depth knowledge. But one should always aim for a certain amount of adaptability — you never know when it will come in useful.

The most important part of any ritual is its *intention*. It is simply no use at all getting everything together, and then trying to decide what you are going to do with it all. Treat these rituals with respect. They are not for your amusement, but for your guidance. None are of long duration, for it is a fallacy that the longer the ritual the better the effect. Neither does it improve your chances if you make every rite as elaborate as possible. Turning simple and effective work into an extravaganza will not help: indeed, it will hinder you.

You will find no mention of the tools of the magician in this book. They are things to make in the future, if and when you decide to go deeper into the Mysteries. Too many magical instruments are made, used once or twice, then left to lie around still charged and capable, in the hands of the wrong or unsuspecting people, of creating havoc. When you do make your instruments, make sure that you also make provision for their destruction in the event of your death. The same goes for robes or Temple equipment you may make in the future. To leave such things lying around is, in an occult sense, unhygienic and irresponsible.

A word of warning here, do not tamper with the rituals in this book, or try to make them more intense or deeper in effect. This is not because I think they cannot be improved; but unless you know what you are doing, you are unlikely to do anything more than unbalance them. If you *do* know what you are doing, then you will not need to study this book. With the exception of the first ritual, which can be used to tap the virtues of any of the Sephiroth of the Tree of Life, they have all been built to ease you gently into this kind of work, and need no embellishment. If you do decide to tinker with them, on your own head be it. This is not a party game. You will be working with your own inner power, so wake it gently. This is the meaning behind the story of the Sleeping Beauty incidentally, which, like all fairy tales, has a bearing on ritual — but that is for another book.

You will need no special equipment, nor will you need a special room in which to perform these rituals. Some of them have been designed for use in the open air. This has a purpose, for until you have worked ritually out of doors, with the wind in your face and the elements about you, you have not touched the height of ritual. I am well aware that there are precious few places with enough privacy to make this possible, but there are a few if you are prepared to search for them. There are also some schools (my own included) who welcome non-students into their ritual training seminars, and these take place in venues where a certain amount of outdoor work is possible. For those of you who would like to take part in such work I have included in this revised edition a list of schools, groups, and organizations who can be contacted for information. This list may be found at the back of the book.

You may be asking yourself why magicians work rituals at all. There are four main reasons; the smaller ones can be left until another time. Firstly, there are rituals that cause effect, either on the physical level or on the subtle levels; healing rituals and those meant to ease ecological disaster, alleviate suffering, weathercraft, and ritual initiation also come into this category. Then there are rituals designed to 'call' objects to you, such as rare books, a new affordable house, a car, or a new job. The third kind uses ritual to tap into one's inner resources and to call out of oneself greater effort: you would use ritual in this sense to encourage self-discipline, increase memory ability, smoothe out character defects, and so on. The last major category of ritual is simply to worship, to blend oneself with the infinite, the Godhead under whatever name you choose to give the Unknowable. You should also understand the difference between *doing* a ritual, *performing* a ritual, and *working* a ritual. 'Doing' indicates that the rite is, in the main, a rehearsal or perhaps to introduce newcomers to the power and pressure of ritual work. 'Performing' a ritual includes ritual drama — not to be taken as being less in power than working a ritual, simply a different way of approaching it. 'Working' a ritual means just that, hard work in its preparation of the place, the self, and the mental and spiritual approach to the task in hand.

How often should ritual work be done? If you are a newcomer then certainly not more than once a month maximum. If pressed, I would say that one simple half-hour ritual, and a longer, more intense ritual in each Tide or Season for a year would be more than enough. However, I have taught magic long enough to realize that few, if any, take notice of such advice. Once a month will not harm you — it will probably teach you more by way of making mistakes than my advice will, anyway.

Make sure you have a bath and wear clean clothes even if you will not be wearing robes. If you are wearing robes, remember when making them to use material that washes. It is amazing how many people clean their Temples and take long cleansing baths before a ritual, but use their robes until they practically drop off them. Either wash them regularly or have them cleaned. These days few cleaners will bat an eyelid at being asked to clean robes.

Incense should be used sparingly. Don't choke yourself with clouds of smoke. Don't unless you are an expert, use a thurible on a swing chain. There is an art to swinging a thurible and, unless you know how to do it, there is a fair chance you will end up with glowing charcoal all over the floor. Most magicians progress to the point of being able to blend their own incenses, but if you do not want to go to the trouble, you can obtain a variety of blends from occult suppliers in almost any big town. Or, enquire from Margaret Bruce at St John's Chapel, Bishop Auckland, Durham, England: Ms Bruce can advise you or even blend a special incense for you.

Remember that ritual is, of itself, only a tool, in the same way that a wand or sword is a tool. It is a means of bringing the heart, mind, body and spirit to the smallest possible point of concentration. Everything about a ritual is designed to increase that concentration — candles, incense, robes, colours, all help the mind to shift levels and work on those levels during the time of the ritual. There will come a time, if you continue your studies, when you will be able to work ritual without a Temple or any kind of magical implement. The Inner Temple will have taken precedence and all work will proceed from there. Later still, you will acquire the ability to shift levels at will and bring the full force of the mind to bear upon the core of any ritual, the *intention*. By fully realizing this intent and making it the central point of your whole multi-level Beingness, you can bring it into manifestation on the physical level. But don't hold your breath, this level can take a lifetime to achieve, and by the time you have achieved it, you will be wise enough not to need anything ritual can give you. Why do it then? Because that is the way you will learn to understand yourself and the universe about you.

For the first ritual in the book, we will aim at something that always needs attention and seldom gets it — self-improvement. This is a solo exercise, and as near disaster-proof as you are likely to get. I have kept the requirements to a minimum, as it will be the actual practice that is the most important thing throughout the book. However, if you already have robes and wish to use them, go ahead. All prayers and invocation are printed in capital letters to make for easy reading in case you want to use the book as a prompter; but it is better, if you can, to memorize the words as this makes for ease of movement and adds to the overall effect of smooth running. One last thing before you start, rituals should be joyful; don't make them into long-faced, over-solemn sessions. If anything goes wrong, simply start again, or backtrack a page and pick up the thread. If it's funny, laugh — you won't get struck down. Laughter is a precious gift at any time, and if ever you are lucky enough to hear the laughter of Gods or Archangels count yourself blessed indeed.

2. THE QABALISTIC TRADITION

RITUAL ONE: INVOKING FOR ORGANIZATION

One of the best things to encourage in oneself is organization. It encompasses a lot of things, all of which will be useful in any future occult work. The framework of the ritual by which we hope to accomplish this self-organization is based upon the Tree of Life, with which many of you will already be familiar. If you are not, then I suggest you start by reading one of the best introductory essays on the Tree ever written, 'The Art of True Healing', by Israel Regardie. This book has been out of print for many years in its early form, but prior to his death in 1985 Dr Regardie combined several of his smaller books into one volume — *Foundations of Practical Magic: An Introduction to Qabalistic, Magical and Meditative Techniques* (Aquarian Press, 1979) — and you can do no better than to obtain this for use as a foundation.

First you need to know where you will be working on the Tree. Chesed, the fourth sphere, is the seat of organization, with emphasis on building, teaching, etc. It is sometimes spoken of as the Sphere of the Masters, or Inner Plane Teachers, whose unenviable task it is to try to improve mankind. Like all the spheres on the Tree, Chesed has a specific magical image for use as a focus for the creative visualization technique. This image is that of a throned and crowned king (see Frontispiece).

All of the Spheres on the Tree work on four levels, which are known as the Four Worlds of the Qabalah. The first of these Worlds is Atziluth, the World of the spiritual level. Here is found the essence of all things; the highest expression possible. A colour is assigned to each Sphere in each World: the colour of Chesed in Atziluth is deep violet. The World of Briah, or the mental aspect, is the next of the Four Worlds, and here the colour we are interested in is deep blue. The third World is named Yetzirah: this is the creative-astral World, its colour being deep purple. The last of the Four Worlds is that of Assiah, the physical

World where all takes shape: here the colour is blue flecked with yellow.

These Four Worlds are all part of the ritual intention. The first World stands for the primal desire or intent, the second for the imprint of this intent upon the mental processes, the third for its prototype on the astral, and the fourth for its appearance on the physical.

It is important that you understand this pattern, and the way in which it works, for upon it all magic is based, no matter what tradition you may be using. This is the strength of the Qabalistic Way, for it is a Cosmic filing system, which once you have learned to use it can be extended to cover any work you might wish to do in the future. All magic, which is merely a pattern of events following Laws that we are still trying to use and understand, works along the same simple line of descent: desire, mental image, astral image, physical formation.

Along with the images and colours, each Sphere has a God name. This is seen as the particular creative aspect of God in that Sphere. The God name of Chesed is *EL*. This name can be found throughout the Bible and other books of Mysteries. It can be found both as a prefix (or root) and as a suffix. EL, among other, more subtle meanings, stands for *GOD*, and we see it occur again on the Tree as Beni ELohim and ELohim Gebor. It appears in most of the Angelic names, MichaEL, GabriEL, RaphaEL, etc. A more comprehensive listing can be found in *The Mystical Qabalah* by Dion Fortune, and the two volumes of *The Practical Guide to Qabalistic Symbolism* by Gareth Knight.

Here is a list of things you will need for this ritual. They are neither expensive, nor hard to obtain:

1. Three packets of crêpe paper, one each of violet, blue and purple, and one packet of round, sticky yellow labels, of the type used in offices for colour coding, in the smallest possible size.

2. A small picture of a king on a throne. If you can draw this yourself, this will be best, as all magical equipment should be made personally if at all possible. If you cannot draw anything better than a matchstick figure, however, then use the Emperor from a Tarot pack, or even the King of Hearts from an ordinary pack of playing cards. (Hearts are cups when translated into the symbolism of the Tarot, and Chesed, like the suit of Cups, is associated with the element of water.) If you do use the Tarot card, remember that in this instance it is used only as a means of focusing on the image of the king; you can forget the usual implications of the card for this ritual.

3. A sheet of stiff card in a deep shade of blue.

4. A small photograph of yourself.

5. A nightlight, similar to those used in a child's room, together with four blue candles and holders.

6. A clean sheet, and a new white handkerchief.

Cut out a square of about 18 inches from the deep violet paper, a smaller one from the deep blue paper, a smaller one still from the purple paper, and finally a little square from the blue paper. Dot the little blue square with some of the yellow sticky circles. You now have the four colours of Chesed in each of the Four Worlds. Exact colours are not always important when you are beginning. Later you might find it necessary to look for exact shades for more important rituals, but for the moment colour is a personal thing and what is violet for you can be something else for the next man. Go by what you feel. Place the four squares on top of each other, so that the border of one is plainly visible all around the one above it. In the centre of the smallest square, pin the picture of the king, and on that the photograph of yourself. Now take the stiff card and cut out four triangles each with a base of 6 inches, a depth of 4 inches, and a side length of 5¾ inches. Tape them together with sticky tape and glue what has now become a pyramid onto a base of the same blue card.

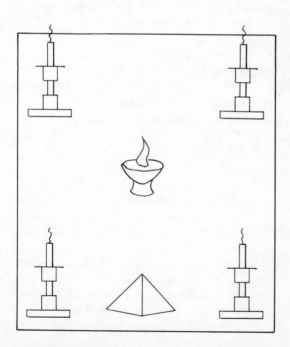

The pyramid is one of the symbols of the Sphere of Chesed, the fourth Sphere, and in fact anything with a connection to the figure four can be used in a ritual dealing with this Sephira. The aim is to have on your temporary altar something representative of the Sphere you are working with.

Now you can start to plan the ritual itself. Privacy is a must, so arrange for the family to be out, or just make sure they know that you are *not* available — for *anything*! Take the telephone off the hook.

If you have no special room for your use, the bedroom will do: working the ritual in your bedroom will not leave undesirable influences around your sleeping area. You are going to work with Angelic forces, not things from a sensational occult novel. Work on a growing (waxing) Moon phase until you have gained the experience and strength to cope with the adverse effects of a waning Moon. A well-trained magician can cope with most phases, lunar or sidereal — in fact it is part of the training to use an adverse phase as a thrust-block — but until such time as you reach that point, use forces that help, not hinder. The saying 'Know Thyself' includes knowing when you are ready to take on the tougher tasks and, more importantly, when you are *not* ready.

Take the clean sheet and spread it out on the floor. You need a working area six-foot square — more if possible. This sheet will represent your Temple for now. Over it, you will erect an Astral Temple, and this will be the real one so far as the working is concerned. The sheet will merely define the place. Put a small table in the middle of the sheet, making sure that you can walk around it without having to step off the sheet or knock anything off the table. Find the four points of the compass, and mark them lightly with chalk. You will be working east to west, and it is important to be correct in this.

Place your Chesedic banner on the eastern wall facing you. Make sure you can see it clearly. Cover the table with the white handkerchief, and in the middle put the nightlight in a holder or saucer. This light is of the greatest importance; it symbolizes the Light of the World, the Divine Child, the Sun behind the Sun, whichever you wish to call it. No ritual should take place in any Temple unless this light is lit. At each corner of the table, place one of the four blue candles. Finally, put the pyramid in front of the central light. The Temple is now ready for use.

The most effective rituals are simple, direct, and to the point; they are not over-long. Hour-long invocations to obscure gods, embellished with dramatic gestures, owe more to Hollywood than to true magic. All such things only serve to inflate the ego, which all egos can do without! It never ceases to amaze me just how many intending magi seem to want to spend most of the ritual slashing around with a large sword. Some rituals by their nature need to be more elaborate than the one you will be doing, but even they rarely last more than an hour and a half to two hours. Extended beyond that, anyone unused to the forces generated at these times will wilt, and that can be not only embarrassing but dangerous as well. Any ritual, at any time, is only as strong as the weakest link among those conducting it. Moral: choose your magical co-workers with great care. When things go wrong, they usually discharge through the weakest member of the group, and the magus. It is uncomfortable to be either in such circumstances.

Cleanliness is important. Take a bath before starting your ritual. Sprinkling the water with salt is an old tradition and certainly helps to cleanse the inner levels. Pay attention to the nails, often neglected in these preparations. Put on clean underwear, white if possible: what to wear over it is no problem. If you have clean nightwear of the right colour (in this case blue), that will be fine. If you have not, then wear whatever is comfortable and clean. You will not get blasted by the powers-that-be if you are not wearing full robes and head-dress. Too much can be made of such things; it is the approach in the mind that matters. As a last resort, just the clean underwear will do. After all, in the past man has performed his rituals in much less — and still does in some cases. You can have the most costly equipment and clothing and still make a mess of the whole thing. Intention is what really matters.

Place a chair inside your Temple in the west and facing the eastern wall and the Chesedic banner. Light the central light, and then light the candles from that light. Take your seat and for a few moments close your eyes and build up around you the Astral Temple of which the simple sheet is the reflection. You can base it on the following description, or you can create your own, but remember — do not make it too elaborate. You should imagine four walls of pale gold, and above the indigo of a night sky, or a golden dome. At each quarter should stand a carved chair. The altar is of black polished wood, covered with a cloth of black silk and an overlay cloth of white. On the altar stands the light and the four candles. The simple pyramid of card becomes a polished crystal of sapphire. The floor is a pavement of black and white marble squares.

Now rise to your feet, and moving deosil go to the east. From there, circle the altar three times, trailing an invisible line of Light after you. Work east to south to west to north, and then back to east. Face the east and raise the right hand, pointing with the first two fingers, and make the Qabalistic Cross, as follows: touch the forehead, and say:

'ATEH.'

Take the fingers down to the solar plexus, and say:
  'MALKUTH.'
Touch the right shoulder and say:
  'VE GEBURAH,'
and then the left shoulder, and say:
  'VE GEDULAH.'
Bring the two hands together and pronounce:
  'LE OLAM, AMEN.'
Now extend the hand to the east and trace in the air an equal-armed cross, and circle it, all in one gesture, saying:
  'IN THE NAME OF ADONAI, I OPEN THE EAST.'
Keeping the hand outstretched, move to the south and repeat the gesture, saying:
  'IN THE NAME OF ADONAI, I OPEN THE SOUTH.'
Repeat this in the west and the north, using the same words with the appropriate compass points. Come back to the east, stand with feet together and arms outstretched, and say:
  'IN THE NAME OF THE LIGHT OF THE WORLD, UNDER THE PROTECTION OF THE GOD NAME EL, I DECLARE THIS TEMPLE OPEN. THE INTENTION TO BE THE AWAKENING WITHIN MY INNER BEING OF THE QUALITY OF ORGANIZATION, ATTRIBUTE OF THE HOLY SPHERE OF CHESED.'
Moving always clockwise, go to your chair in the western quarter, sit down facing the east, and take up the godform meditation position. Excitement may have tensed you up a little, so take a few moments to relax. Start the breathing in a four, two, four rhythm. Fix your attention on the banner on the opposite wall, and concentrate on it totally. Pick out each colour, until you come to the photograph. Now return to the first section of colour, and do it again. At the same time, start to repeat your first name over and over again as you go through the colours. Keep looking at them in sequence, from the outer violet to the inner photograph, still repeating your name. Think of the violet as the primal creative power of Chesed, the spiritual focus of the Sphere, pouring down into the deep blue of the mental level. Identify your name with the Chesedic ability to bring about order, and let it spill over into the purple section, coming into the lower astral levels. Now tip the whole lot into the blue, yellow-flecked area, and fill up the image of the king. Once you have got this far, link name, king and your photograph together, and let it all centre on the photograph. This now becomes the focal point of all that is flowing down from the highest point of Chesed. You are the recipient of the whole flow of organizing

power. Just the getting together of everything that was needed to do the ritual is part of that power, so right from the start you have been using it unawares. Your own inner kingship is opening up and filling with the blended colours. The Four Worlds are concentrated on that one small picture. Do not try to keep it all separate. Let it melt into one, an alchemical process of progression and fulfilment.

Keeping the thought as steady as you can, rise and move round to the east to face the altar. Stand with arms outstretched, head tilted a little back. You are now ready for the next phase. Keeping the image of the power-filled photograph in your mind's eye, exert your will, and *pull* that image down off the wall and toward the heart centre. Use every bit of your imagination to see it coming toward you, entering the body through the spinal column, and moving into the heart centre. There let it change into an intense blue flame that fills the entire body. Start to repeat your name again, equating it with the blue flame that is now awakening the inherent quality of organization within you. Now pick up the pyramid, and flow into it some of the blue radiance that fills you. Fill it right up and then seal it by imagining the circled cross on each of its four sides.

Replace it on the altar. Take up the Light, and lift it to eye level, saying:
'THUS DO I LIFT UP MY HEART, MY MIND AND MY SPIRIT TO THE LIGHT. LET THE DIVINE WILL AND MINE BE AS ONE.'
Replace the Light, and turn to the east again. Repeat the Qabalistic Cross as in the beginning, then repeat the tracing of the sigils at the points, each time closing them with the words:
'IN THE NAME OF ADONAI, I CLOSE THE . . .'
Go back to the altar and give ten spaced knocks on the table, saying:
'IN THE NAME OF THE LIGHT OF THE WORLD, I DECLARE THIS TEMPLE CLOSED, AND THE RITE ENDED.'
To end, retrace the three circles, anti-clockwise, rewinding the light within yourself. Put out the four blue candles, and finally the altar light. The ritual is completed.

I have reduced this little ceremony to its essentials, not even using the Archangelic names and forms. Working under the God name and the Light means you have all the protection you need at this time. It is important, once you have completed the ritual, to have something to eat and drink, even though you may not feel like it. This closes down the centres you have opened up and prevents any backlash. Before you sleep, write down your impressions of the ritual, noting where you thought it could have been better, or if it felt particularly good. Take note on the days following of any effects that occur on the physical levels.

It is also as well to get into the habit of keeping a diary of all the work that you do, together with anything you come across that affects you — a sentence or a piece of poetry, a passing idea or thought. Do not say, 'Oh, I'll remember that', because it is a pound of frankincense to an ounce of myrrh that you will not. So write it down. It will build up over the months and years, and looking back over it will enable you not only to judge your progress, but will make up the sum of your knowledge as you grow in understanding. Besides this, all those who enter the Mysteries have the onus placed upon them to train someone to come after. These books of your own work will be of great value to them.

This ritual may be adapted to any of the Spheres of the Tree, using the colours and images and symbols given for that Sphere. To get the full effect, it should be performed once a week from New Moon to Full, using the dark quarter to meditate on them. Better still, work a full Tide of three months. Do not expect results overnight; it takes time to change things. You must not hope to become Vice-President of the company on the strength of one ritual. Everything grows from the inner levels toward the outer, so the first sign will be when you find your own inner life and thoughts becoming placed in neat rows.

As you can see, a ritual is possible without expensive equipment, or even a special room for a Temple. They are nice to have, but by no means essential. To be able to work ceremonial magic with little or nothing in the way of an aid is the mark of a well-trained and highly efficient magician. It is also the way of the Aquarian Age and the new coming stage in the Mysteries. Even now, teachers and students are starting to use their minds alone to work ritual and, as I have said, the physical plane Temple may soon be a thing of the past, though it will always be a beautiful and rewarding experience to use one. However, the new method is gradually coming into practice, and highly-trained occultists are beginning to gather together to work entire rituals on the inner levels, using only the mind and its incredible imaginative powers. Of course, there will be no overnight change; the Temple will be with us for a long time yet, and indeed there will always be a place for rituals worked in the old ways. However, change *must* come to the Mysteries like any other system, and as men and women uncover the abilities that have been hidden for so long we shall see many changes. There will be those who resist them, but come they must.

RITUAL TWO: EMPOWERING YOUR DREAMS

If working with the Qabalah it is useful to note that the most fruitful rituals are those using three of the spheres. Working with just one, as in Ritual One, certainly creates an effect, but working with two in balance is even better. However, it is when the interaction between two spheres is used to push an effect through a third that you start to realize the latent power lying hidden in the symbol of the Tree of Life.

At first the easiest triangles to use are those that occur naturally, i.e. Malkuth, Hod and Netzach, or Yesod, Hod and Netzach. This can be extended to Hod, Tiphereth and Netzach, and on to Geburah, Tiphereth and Chesed, and so on. Later, when the Tree has become part of your life, needing no effort to recall its symbols, correspondences, and formations, you can stretch the triangles further apart. This means you could use Binah, Hod and Chesed, or Malkuth, Kether and Tiphereth, as the 'working' point of the ritual. This second ritual along Qabalistic lines will use Malkuth and Netzach as the basal line of the triangle and Yesod as the working point. If you look at the picture on page 26. You will see that these three spheres make a natural triangle.

The intention of the ritual is to empower your dreams, to make them clearer, easier to remember in the morning, and to increase the value of their content. We need to begin with looking at the spheres themselves, their symbols, colours, and correspondences.

MALKUTH is the level of earth, or ASSIAH in the Four Worlds (see Qabalistic Ritual One), the level where you will need to remember your dreams in the morning. In Atziluth, Malkuth's colour is yellow, while in Briah the colours are citrine, olive, russet and black, and in Yetzirah (where this ritual will be working) they are the same but with flecks of gold in the black. In the world of Assiah, the physical level, the colours are black rayed with yellow. The Tarot cards associated with Malkuth are the *Tens* of the suits: Ten of Wands = oppression, Ten of Cups = perfected success, Ten of Swords = ruin, and Ten of Pentacles = wealth. The usual altar symbol for earth is salt in a small container. This is by no means the end of the list, but it is all you need to know for this ritual. The Archangel is Sandalphon.

NETZACH is the sphere of Venus, and of creative power and the diversity of life in all its forms. It is, together with Yesod, the sphere of magical power which is always linked to the creative sexual power in mankind. Its colours are for the most part variations on green. At the Atziluthic level the colour is amber, and at the level of Briah this

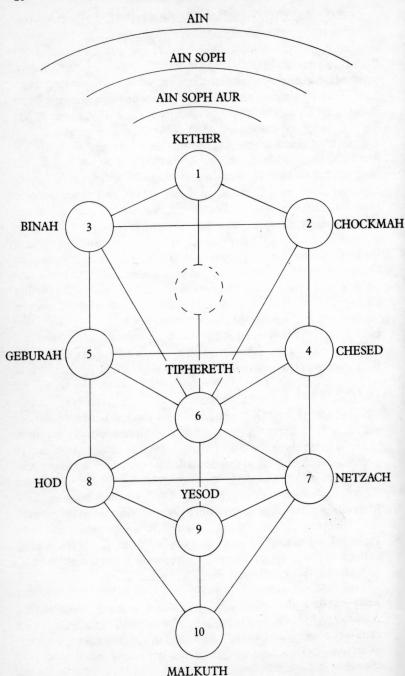

changes to emerald. In Yetzirah it is a bright yellowish green, and then in Assiah an olive green flecked with gold. The Tarot cards for Netzach are the *Sevens*: Seven of Wands = valour, Seven of Cups = illusory success, Seven of Swords = unstable effort, and Seven of Pentacles = success unfulfilled. The usual symbol for Netzach is a rose or a small lamp; the rose is better as it poses no danger if knocked off the altar by accident. The Archangel is named Haniel.

YESOD, lastly, is the sphere of the Moon. It is sometimes called the Treasure House of Images — it is the sphere of dreams and also of great strength, for dreams used with power can materialize in Malkuth. This sphere like Netzach is creative and holds power of an unimaginable kind and therefore needs to be treated with respect. Like the Moon it has two faces and you can easily find yourself looking at the wrong one. At the Atziluthic level Yesod's colour is indigo, at the level of Briah it turns to violet, then changes to dark purple in Yetzirah's level, and then citrine flecked with blue in Assiah. Its symbols are perfumes and the sacred sandals — incense of course can act as the perfume in this instance, but because Yesod is connected with water a chalice will be just as appropriate. The Archangel is Gabriel.

With this information to hand you can choose what you will need. First of all, candles. As we will be working towards an effect on the astral level the colours in each case will need to be the astral colours: for Netzach, a yellowish green (if this is difficult to find use a yellow candle and use a green pen or crayon to add some green tones); for Yesod, a dark purple; and for Malkuth, you have a choice of citrine, olive, russet red, or black flecked with gold — the russet red or olive will probably be the easiest to buy. Any Lunar incense will do — it will probably have some camphor in it somewhere — and you will need a single rose, a small container of salt, and a little red wine in a chalice (if you do not have one, a clean, polished glass will do just as well). As in the first ritual of this type you will need a clean sheet to mark off a 'sacred space' and a small table covered with a clean white cloth to act as an altar. A chair in which to sit before the altar completes all that you need for this ritual.

Put down the sheet and smoothe it out as far as possible, using whatever space you have — don't be afraid to improvise if working in a small room. Such simple rituals as these, which do not need a lot of movement, can be used even in a bedsitter. Use the same preparations as for the Chesedic ritual — i.e. bathe and put on clean clothes. Set your altar with the centre light and arrange the three candles in their holders so that they form a triangle around it. Put the dark purple candle in front of you, forming the apex of the triangle. The russet or olive candle of Malkuth goes to the back left-hand side of the altar, with the salt just in front of it, and the yellow/green Netzach candle at the back and to the right, with the rose in front of it. The incense burner goes at the back between the two candles. The chalice stands to your right beside the Yesod (but not so close that it can get knocked over). Beneath each candle put a Tarot card covered by a piece of greaseproof paper to protect it. Beneath the candle of Netzach place the Seven of Wands for valour. Beneath the candle of Malkuth put the Ten of Cups for perfected success, and under the candle of Yesod place the Nine of Wands, meaning great strength. All these will serve to concentrate the mind on the task at hand.

As with Ritual One, sit in silence facing the altar for a few minutes, in your imagination building the Astral Temple over the simple layout you have put together. Use the same images with walls of pale gold, a night sky overhead, the quarter furnishings, and on the altar the three candles, the altar light, etc. If you have room to move, rise to your feet and circle the sacred space deosil three times. If there is no room for this then just stand and make the Qabalistic Cross, then follow the gestures and words according to the first ritual until you return to the east. Now, stand with feet together and arms outstretched and say:

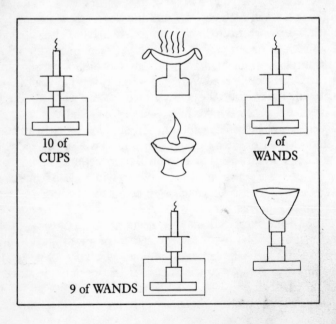

10 of CUPS

7 of WANDS

9 of WANDS

'IN THE NAME OF THE LORDS OF LIGHT AND UNDER THE PROTECTION OF SHADDAI EL CHAI, I DECLARE THIS TEMPLE OPEN. THE RITUAL INTENT: TO CHANNEL THE CREATIVE POWER OF NETZACH AND THE RECEPTIVE POWER OF MALKUTH INTO THE SPHERE OF YESOD, THAT MY DREAMS MAY BE TOUCHED BY INNER WISDOM, AND BE HELD SECURE IN THE WAKING MEMORY.'

Take your seat again and fix your eyes upon the candle of Netzach; recall what you know about this Sephira, that it is the sphere of love and of life in all its many forms. It is a sphere of creative power and you are going to pull that power down through the inner levels and into the flame of the candle. In your mind's eye see the power of the Venus sphere as a beam of brilliant green light pouring into the flame of the candle. If you are one of the few people who cannot visualize, think the image instead of seeing it. As the light continues to fill up the flame you can begin to see shapes and forms in the flickering light; flowers and animal forms, tiny winged figures that seem surrounded by glowing light; cats' eyes and pearls, rose petals and faces of gold-like men and women from the ancient pantheons. Continue until you feel you cannot pack another thing into the flame. Go to the altar and pass your hand over the flame of the yellow-green candle three times saying:

'I PLACE THE SEAL OF THIS TEMPLE UPON THE CANDLE OF NETZACH, LET THIS BE WITNESSED BY THE PRESENCE OF HANIEL.'

Return to your seat.

Now concentrate on the candle of Malkuth in the same way. This is the sphere of form, of physical life, and it links with the sphere of Netzach in that physical love calls into being new physical forms. Into this flame you must pour the most beautiful things of this level, not just of form but also of mind. Think of your favourite soothing music, the faces of your loved ones, sites of great beauty and peace that may be familiar to you — things you have heard or read that have helped you to understand the world in which you live. Above all, fill the flame with the idea of being able to receive and learn new ideas and concepts. When you have finished get up and go to the altar and perform the sealing again, this time over the candle of Malkuth, saying:

'I PLACE THE SEAL OF THIS TEMPLE UPON THE CANDLE OF MALKUTH, LET THIS BE WITNESSED BY THE PRESENCE OF SANDALPHON.'

Return to your seat.

Now it is the turn of the candle of Yesod. It is the white and silver sphere of dreams and of the Moon. Just look deeply into the flame of this candle and let your mind become one with it; let the dreamer part of you melt with the flame and dance with it. Let your dreams, hopes, thoughts, desires, and wishes fill the flame until it overflows. Now get up and at the altar seal the flame, saying:

'I PLACE THE SEAL OF THIS TEMPLE UPON THE CANDLE OF YESOD, LET THIS BE WITNESSED BY THE PRESENCE OF GABRIEL.'

Take the wine and put into it a tiny pinch of salt, and one petal from the rose, place it before you on the altar and pass over it the burning incense, saying:

'WITH BURNING HERBS BOTH BITTER AND SWEET I PURIFY AND HALLOW THIS CUP OF WINE.'

Replace the incense and pass the wine over the centre light, saying:

'WITH THE INFINITE LIGHT I BLESS AND HALLOW THIS CUP OF WINE, MAY THAT WITHIN IT BE FILLED WITH LIGHT, AND THAT WHICH TAKES IT IN BE HALLOWED BY THAT LIGHT.'

Replace cup on the altar.

Take up the candle of Netzach and pass it over the incense:

'I CLEANSE ALL THAT LIES WITHIN THIS FLAME AND HALLOW IT TO MY PURPOSE.'

Pass candle over the centre light:

'I BLESS ALL THAT LIES WITHIN THIS FLAME AND HALLOW IT TO MY PURPOSE.'

Turn candle over and plunge the flame into the wine.

Take up the candle of Malkuth and pass it over the incense:

'I CLEANSE ALL THAT LIES WITHIN THIS FLAME AND HALLOW IT TO MY PURPOSE.'

Pass candle over the centre light:

'I BLESS ALL THAT LIES WITHIN THIS FLAME AND HALLOW IT TO MY PURPOSE.'

Turn the candle over and plunge the flame into the wine.

Now take up the candle of Yesod and pass it over the incense:

'I CLEANSE ALL THAT LIES WITHIN THIS FLAME AND HALLOW IT TO MY PURPOSE.'

Pass it over the centre light:

'I BLESS ALL THAT LIES WITHIN THIS FLAME AND HALLOW IT TO MY PURPOSE.'

Turn the candle over and plunge the flame into the wine.

Lift the cup up and over the centre light and say:

'I CALL THEE HANIEL, ARCHANGEL OF NETZACH TO

WITNESS AS I PLEDGE THEE AND THE SPHERE OVER
WHICH THOU HAST BEEN GIVEN LORDSHIP.'
Drink a little wine:
  'THUS DO I TAKE INTO MYSELF THE POWER OF
NETZACH.'
Lift the cup again over and above the centre light:
  'I CALL THEE SANDALPHON, ARCHANGEL OF
MALKUTH TO WITNESS AS I PLEDGE THEE AND THE
SPHERE OVER WHICH THOU HAST BEEN GIVEN
LORDSHIP.'
Drink some of the wine:
  'THUS DO I TAKE INTO MYSELF THE POWER OF
MALKUTH.'
And again lift the cup over the centre light.
  'I CALL THEE GABRIEL, ARCHANGEL OF YESOD TO
WITNESS AS I PLEDGE THEE AND THE SPHERE OVER
WHICH THOU HAST BEEN GIVEN LORDSHIP.'
Drink the rest of the wine:
  'THUS DO I TAKE INTO MYSELF THE POWER OF YESOD
AND THE POWER OF MY DREAMS. SO MOTE IT BE THIS
NIGHT.'
Replace the cup and bow to the centre light:
  'I CALL UPON THE TEACHERS OF THE INNER LEVELS
TO SPEAK TO ME IN MY DREAMS THAT I MAY LEARN AND
GROW IN WISDOM AND IN UNDERSTANDING. GUIDE ME
AND GUARD ME AND MAKE OF ME ONE WHO WILL BE
WORTHY OF THY TEACHING.'
  Return to your seat and sit in silence for a little while, allowing your
inner self to assimilate all that has been offered to it. Then return to
the altar and lift the light high, saying:
  'HOLY ART OH LORD OF THE UNIVERSE
  HOLY ART THOU WHOM NATURE HATH NOT FORMED
  HOLY ART THOU OH VAST AND MIGHTY ONE
  LORD OF THE LIGHT AND LORD OF THE DARKNESS
  HERE I STAND OH LORD
  I OFFER MYSELF TO BE
  A HOLY AND CONTINUING SACRIFICE UNTO THEE.'
Replace the light and, facing east, make the Qabalistic Cross and
then repeat the tracing of the sigils as you did at the beginning of the
ritual at all four quarters, saying:
  'IN THE NAME OF ADONAI I CLOSE THE . . .'
Return to the altar and knock nine times upon it, in three lots of three
(nine being the number of Yesod):

'IN THE NAME OF THE LORDS OF LIGHTS AND OF SHADDAI EL CHAI I DECLARE THIS TEMPLE CLOSED AND THE RITE ENDED.'

Allow the centre light to burn for a little while and then put it out and clear everything away. Sit down and have something hot to drink and a biscuit to help you close down. It is a good idea to go to bed and sleep within the hour, then write up your notes after 24 hours. From now on keep a pad and pen by your pillow and write down your dreams as soon as you wake up. After about a week start to act upon any inner directive your dreams may be suggesting. Research a symbol that keeps recurring, look up godforms that may appear and make sure you know the myths and correspondences pertaining to them. From then on you can start trying to direct your dreams by meditating upon a subject or figure immediately prior to sleeping.

3. THE EGYPTIAN TRADITION

RITUAL ONE: THE MEETING OF MIND WITH MIND

Egyptian magic is in a class of its own. Unless you are fully conversant with its complex system of godforms and mythology, a full-scale ritual is out of the question, even with a fully equipped temple. However, it is possible to adapt some of the methods to produce a rite that is both emotionally satisfying and true to type.

The Mysteries of the Land of Khem are as rich and varied as its beliefs. It has been said that from its name came the word we know as alchemy, and that the word 'Khem' means black. Another source offers the explanation that the word has been confused with another, meaning wise. Imperfect knowledge of the ancient tongues and the ways in which they were pronounced — and of course, the inclusion of local idiom during translation — has left us with many such problems. This being so, we must use what we have in the best possible way and hope that the old gods will understand our strange pronounciation.

Egypt holds a special place in ritual magic because, for one thing, it is more mentally orientated. The Orphic rite, which we shall be trying in Chapter 4 was a joyous exaltation of mind, body and spirit; the Celtic was as deep and mysterious as an underground stream of sweet water; but the ancient Egyptian was more concerned with the life of the spirit than that of the body, and so the Priests of Khem sought to endow that part of themselves with power more than any other level. This held true until a time came, as it does with all traditions, when earthly power seduced them from their path; but when the priest-kings ruled in the early dynasties, the priests reached a very high level indeed in their work, and some of their rituals are still available to those able to work them. However for our present purpose they are too advanced. We need something that, just for a short time, will bring us into contact with one of the best-known and best-loved archetypal figures of the Egyptian Mysteries.

The worship of the Great Mother has never ceased, and never will. Her name may change from time to time, but Her essence remains with us. Men and women alike seek Her, each in their own way. For women, this brings a sense of identification with the archetypal feminine aspect. For men, contact with Her brings a sense of wonder they never lose thereafter; in their deepest sorrows, their greatest pleasures, and at the moment of death, Her name is most often on their lips. All gods are one God, say the occultists, and all the goddesses one Goddess. Of the latter, none is more beautiful or rewarding to work with than the godform of the Great Mother Isis.

This archetype was chosen for two reasons; the form is easy to build up in the mind — even after centuries of change and adaptation it is still readily available to us, since the idea of the Mother is universal — and it is also one of the safest archetypes for a beginner to use. Like all mothers, Isis is inclined to be indulgent with her children when they reach up to touch Her.

The ritual is designed for a man and a woman working together and is adapted from a much longer one that was once part of the Grade Rituals of the Priesthood of Isis in the City of On. In the old scripts it is called the 'Meeting of Mind with Mind'. Here the priestess takes on the presence of Isis for a short time to enable her companion priest to make his contact with the Goddess. It takes a lot of practice, and some preparation, but if you are persistent the meeting will be effected in time. There is nothing dangerous in it, unlike the rituals of the much higher Grades that followed it. You cannot come to any greater harm than a headache.

Prepare your place of working by first making sure you will not be disturbed. As in the Qabalistic ritual a large clean sheet will be needed to act as the Temple floor. A small table covered with a white cloth will do for an altar and you will need either blue or orange candles, for you will be working in the sphere of the mind. Three candles are needed, for that is the number of the Mother in her form aspect. If you can use incense without disturbing others, use Kyphi if you can get it. If you cannot, you can make use of pine needles with resin and some lavender.

Use the same kind of altar light as in the last chapter — a night-light in a heat-resistant bowl. Because the Mother is the chalice of life, the light for her is always in a container, thus symbolizing the Divine Child within the Mother. Having bathed and dressed (white or blue robes if you have them, just clean clothes, if not), light the charcoal and get it glowing. Arrange the three candles in a triangle about the altar flame and, lastly, put the incense to the charcoal. In this rite, the quarters are guarded by four godforms in a specific order. They are not those of the original ritual, for those would generate too powerful a presence. Therefore instead of four aspects of Isis you will use only two, plus the two half-brothers, Horus and Anubis, with whom Isis is usually associated.

Now the ritual itself may start. Both priest and priestess stand in front of the altar. The priestess lights first the altar light, and from it the three candles. She then places both hands on the altar, face down. The priest, standing behind her, raises his hands, palms outwards. They speak together, saying:

'THOU WHO ART THE MOTHER OF ALL THINGS, WHOSE SON IS THE SUN, COME FROM THY FAR OFF PLACE AND WALK AMONG US WHO ART THY CHILDREN. COME FROM THE HALLS OF ON TO BE OUR TEACHER AND OUR GUIDE. LOOK WITH FAVOUR UPON SHE WHO IS THY PRIESTESS AND MAKE HER THY GARMENT, AND UPON HE WHO WOULD BE THY PRIEST AND OPEN THE STAR CENTRE OF ISIS WITHIN THE PRIESTESS TO HIM, THAT HE MAY KNOW THEE IN THE MIND.'

Note that both participants should be to the east, facing west. Normally a priestess opening her centre to the Goddess would work from west to east, allowing the influence to come in through the nape of the neck. Here, however, we have the male personality standing behind her during the ritual, and so the entry point of the goddess will be through the throat centre and up through the roof of the soft palate into the area of the limbic system. Entry from either the nape of the neck or the throat ends up in the same area. There should also be a small chair for the priestess to sit on if she is as tall as the priest. It is important that she be at least half a head lower than him during the ritual. This chair may be set at the side of the Temple and fetched when needed.

The priest can now open the Temple. Facing the Eastern Gate, he should raise both arms, and say:

'LIGHT OF RA, FILL ME WITH THY RADIANCE THAT I MAY OPEN THIS PLACE OF WORSHIP.'

Here he should point with his forefinger to the east, building in his mind's eye a point of intense light from which will grow concentric circles in a continuous stream. He should then say:

'TO THE EAST I SUMMON HORUS, THE HAWK OF THE SUN, TO GUIDE AND GUARD THIS PLACE OF WORKING'.

Moving to the south, and without lowering his finger, he should repeat the sigil, and say:

'TO THE SOUTH I SUMMON ANUBIS, WHO WALKS IN BOTH THE LIGHT AND THE DARKNESS WITHOUT FEAR. THE JACKAL OF THE DESERTS OF THE MIND, BRING TRUTH TO THIS PLACE OF WORKING.'

He should then move to the west and repeat the opening sign, saying:

'TO THE WEST I SUMMON HATHOR, LADY OF JOY AND BRINGER OF LIFE, TO MAKE THIS PLACE OF WORKING FRUITFUL IN ALL ITS ENDEAVOURS.'

Moving to the north he should again repeat the sign, and say:

'IN THE NORTH I SUMMON NEPTHYS THE COMFORTER, THAT SHE MAY BRING STRENGTH TO THIS PLACE OF WORKING.'

The priest should now take his place behind the priestess, and she, if seated, rises for her prayer, resuming her seat at the end of it, as follows:

'GREAT ISIS, BEHOLD THY HANDMAIDEN WAITS FOR THY PRESENCE. MAKE ME THY GARMENT FOR A SHORT SPACE OF TIME; A HALL WHERE GODDESS AND PRIEST MAY MEET MIND TO MIND. IT IS HIS WISH TO KNOW THE MIND OF THE MOTHER THAT CAN AWAKEN IN HIM THE KNOWLEDGE OF THY ETERNAL PRESENCE IN THE HEART OF EVERY MAN. MAKE HIM FREE OF THE STAR CENTRE THAT IS THE HOUSE OF ISIS IN EVERY PRIESTESS. FOR ME THY PRESENCE IS REWARD ENOUGH.'

Whether the priestess is sitting or standing, the following instructions are the same. She should raise both hands, palms outward, thumbs on a level with the ears. The priest should place both his hands on hers, with his palms covering the backs of her hands. She should then cross her arms, the priest still following, until they lie on the upper part of her chest. The priest's thumbs should now be touching the pulse points on either side of her neck. If he does not feel the pulse beats immediately he should move the thumbs slightly until he can feel them. The priest should make himself deeply conscious of those pulse beats, letting them become a beat in his mind. His task is then to align his own heartbeats with those of the priestess, so that they work as one. Normally, a woman's heartbeat during ritual is quicker than that of a man. It is part of the ritual that these be matched.

During this time, the priestess should go deep within herself, drawing the Isis power to her from the Western Gate, through her throat and up into the region of the pituitary gland. It is important that she does not allow her head to sink down or the line of direction will be lost. Keep the head erect. The area to be energized is the Star Centre, sometimes called the Hall of Isis, and the priestess should see it as a

The Star Chamber of Isis

great hall deep within her. This is where a garment of Isis meets with her Goddess, and it should be seen as filled with a silvery light that emanates from all around. Here the priestess must now build up the presence of the Goddess. This is what takes much practice. No teacher in the world can show you how it is done. It comes only from your own desire and need to experience it: it may happen the first time you attempt it, it may take much longer. When She arrives, you will know. It can be a shock, sharing your body with something, particularly something which although stepped down in power is nevertheless part of an immensely powerful archetype. When she feels the moment is right, the priestess should signal to the priest that he may begin the entry. This can be done by a slight pressure of the hand.

For his part, the priest must now through his will extend a thread of light from the pineal centre down through the back of the priestess' head and into the Hall prepared for his meeting with the Goddess. It is a good idea to study the diagram below in order to have a clear idea of the areas in which you should be working. When the thread of alignment has been established, the second part of the exercise may be attempted. The consciousness of the priest must now be sent along this thread until he is able to stand within the Hall of the Star Centre.

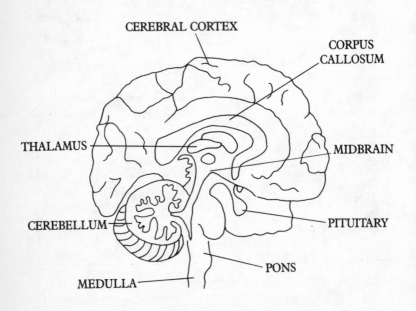

Areas of the Brain

Here a contact can be made with the Goddess if the desire and dedication is there. The contact is a very personal one, and it will differ from person to person. It leads, in time, to a knowledge of the anima within, something that can bring lasting benefit and great understanding to those experiencing the Mind Touch of the Goddess. As a woman, I cannot tell you what it feels like, but it has been described to me as 'a feeling of being surrounded by stars', and again, 'as if I were a musical instrument whose strings were being plucked by an unknown hand'. When it happens, you will know it, but do not expect it to happen right away. It can take time before the Mind Touch comes. You will also know when it is time to withdraw. There comes a moment when you can tell for certain that the Goddess is no longer there. You must then take care to withdraw slowly, or your priestess will end up with a migraine. Use the same road back, and settle within your own centre of awareness, making sure that you can see, hear, feel and balance.

You should then make sure that your partner also gets back into her own world. Wait until the pressure of her hands on yours tells you that she is self-aware. Then slowly uncross her arms, moving together gracefully, and taking your time. Once in the original position, the priest should take his hands from those of his partner, and both participants should return their arms to their sides. Wait for a moment before you start the last part of the ritual. Never hurry any part of a ritual. Let it all come from within. Every moment, every gesture, should be the result of *your* decision, consciously expressed. The first reaction after ritual may be tiredness, but this will be only temporary. If ritual makes you so tired that you cannot cope with your everyday work, then something is wrong.

At this point, it is time to offer thanks, and to close the Temple. The priestess should therefore place both her hands on the altar again, and say:

'GREAT MOTHER, I THANK THEE FOR WHAT THOU HAS GRANTED TO ME, THY HANDMAIDEN. IT IS MY DELIGHT TO BE THY GARMENT, AND TO SERVE THEE IN THY PURPOSE. TO THEE MY PRAISE AND MY SERVICE.'

Then the priest should say:

'FOR THE GIFT OF THIS MEETING WITH THEE, I GIVE THANKS GREAT ISIS. TO THEE MY PRAISE AND MY SERVICE.'

Both priest and priestess should then turn to the east, and say together:

'PRAISE BE TO THAT WHICH IS GIVEN TO ALL MEN, THE LIGHT BY WHICH WE MAY FOLLOW AND BE LED. PRAISE TO THAT LIGHT WHICH IS HELD IN THE HEARTS OF ALL

MEN, AND BY WHICH WE COME TO THE HALLS OF OSIRIS RISEN.'

The priest may now close the Temple, using the same sigil and words with which he opened it, except that instead of summoning, he should now give the godforms permission to depart. Lastly, he should face the altar and declare the Temple closed, put out the candles, and lastly put out the light. Then it is time to have something to eat and drink, and set down the record of the ritual. Do this while it is still fresh in the mind. You have both used centres within that you may never have used before.

This is not an easy ritual. It can take a few times to get it right on the performance level, let alone feel the inner effect of it. On the other hand, it has been known to take effect the first time, much to the surprise of those concerned. It needs, and will increase, a rapport between you and your partner, so choose that partner carefully. It also tends to open a slight telepathic link as well. It will in the end bring about a recognition between the priest and his anima, something which can be of great value to him in future workings of all kinds. It can also enable him, once the link is established, to use the anima as a priestess, it being extruded for this purpose in the form of the Goddess; but this is High Magic, and something to aim for in the future. It also carries a certain risk for the unwary and the profane. Worked with dedication and a genuine desire to contact the Isis godform, it can bring about an unforgettable experience.

RITUAL TWO: THE RITE OF BROTHERHOOD

One of the seminars I am most consistently asked to give is called 'The Women's Mysteries'. This is purely for women, men not being allowed — not to be devisive, but because each sex has it own Mysteries and rituals as well as those that are enjoyed together. The Men's Mysteries are just as powerful and as satisfying to them and carry a magical charge that is just as powerful.

It is impossible when one is involved with magical ritual as deeply as I am not be be aware of what goes on in the opposite camp. Among the hundreds of rituals that have come into my hands over the years is a fragment of paper, a mere two pages, of a ritual for four men. Its tradition is unknown, its author long since passed to Amenti in the west. No god-names are given, so I have transposed it into the Egyptian style. By writing via my animus rather than, as is usual, through my own female self, I hope I have managed to present a ritual for men that they will enjoy working. Consider it a gift to all men of a magical persuasion that comes with affection from a woman who has always enjoyed their company. I might add that to balance things I have included an all-women ritual later in the book.

From the scant information I have it would appear that the ritual is worked in a spiral format. I have kept to this by using a set of godforms that offer a spiral relationship between them. In Egyptian mythology Geb is an earth godform and by his sister Nut or Nuit he is the father of Osiris, Isis, Set and Nephthys. He is depicted as ithyphallic, symbolizing his generative powers, and is an exception to the often-held rule that the earth is female. Osiris, the son of Geb, is one of the main and best known godforms of Ancient Egypt; he is the father of Anubis by his younger sister Nephthys, and of Horus by his twin sister Isis. Thus in this ritual you have the three generations of gods. It might also be worked by using the four sons of Horus who traditionally guarded the four canopic jars used to hold the organs removed from a body prior to embalming.

The intention of this ritual is to bring four men into a firm bonding that can become closer than the relationship between blood kin. I know that women will be tempted to work it for their own rites, but a little gentle advice — don't; please use the one I have written for you further into the book. If you were to try this rite you might think it had worked, but it can mess up the endocrine system and disturb the balance of the female hormones.

This ritual should really be worked in a Temple, or at least in a room large enough in which to move around. However, it can be done in the mind as a pathworking if you are unable to comply with the requirements. If you do have a sacred space and want to do it in true ritual style, you might like to make up four Egyptian collars (see the instructions at the end of the chapter) and instead of robes use white cloth or even a white towel wrapped around the hips and secured at the side. This gives a fairly accurate Egyptian-style kilt. (If you would like to use ritual masks for the Jackal and the Hawk and you live within reach of the London area, there is a shop called 'The Theatre Zoo' in Earlham Street that sells animal masks. While you will not find a jackal, you can use a fox mask, spraying it black and outlining the eyes Egyptian fashion in gold; attach a nemyss of gold/black and gold to the back of the mask. You will have to cut away the base of the mask to enable you to be heard clearly. You can make yourself a hawk head

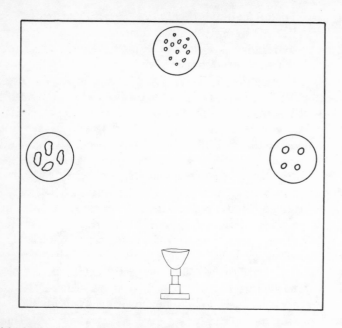

with, believe it or not, a parrot or a puffin mask, sprayed with gold and the eyes outlined. Attach a gold nemyss, and with the pectoral collars the whole thing will look quite authentic.)

You will need a small table, covered with a white cloth, for an altar, on which you place four pieces of bread — each sprinkled with a pinch of salt — on a small plate to the north, a small bowl of sweetcorn to the east, four small gold-coloured coins to the south, and a chalice of wine to the west. In the centre of the altar stand a bowl of burning incense — Kyphi is the most appropriate. Before the ritual begins the four will take their places, Geb sitting in the north, Osiris sitting in the east, Horus sitting in the south and Anubis in the west. The ritual begins with the assumption of their respective godforms by the four men, allow a full five minutes for this. Geb stands and faces north, raising his hands to shoulder height, palms outward.

Geb: 'THE NORTH IS THE PLACE OF GREATEST POWER, I OPEN THIS PLACE BY MY WILL AND WITH THE GESTURE OF POWER.'
(Places left-hand palm open over heart and holds the right arm, palm open and at right-angles to wrist, out in front of him, then turns to face east and holds out hands palms upwards.)

'TAKE THE THREAD OF LIGHT MY BROTHER AND OPEN THE EAST.'

Osiris: (Stands and comes to Geb laying his hands on his, then turns and goes to stand facing east.)

'THE EAST IS THE PLACE OF THE DAWN AND OF ETERNAL LIFE. I OPEN THIS PLACE BY MY WILL AND WITH THE GESTURE OF THE SUN ARISING.'

(Makes circle with forefingers and thumbs, and lifts this symbol slowly up, to just over his head. Then turns to face south, hands out, palms upwards.)

'TAKE THE THREAD OF LIGHT MY BROTHER AND OPEN THE SOUTH.'

Horus: (Stands and comes to Osiris, laying his hands on his, then turns and goes to stand facing south.)

'THE SOUTH IS THE PLACE OF THE SUN AT NOON AND OF COURAGE AND LOYALTY. I OPEN THIS PLACE BY MY WILL AND WITH THE GESTURE OF BROTHERHOOD.'

(Holds out arms and grasps each wrist with the opposite hand. Then turns to face west, holding out his hands, palms upwards.)

'TAKE THE THREAD OF LIGHT MY BROTHER, AND OPEN THE WEST.'

Anubis: (Stands and comes to Horus, laying his hands on his, then turns and goes to stand facing west.)

'THE WEST IS THE PLACE OF DEATH AND DREAMS AND THE ULTIMATE TRUTH. I OPEN THIS PLACE BY MY WILL AND WITH THE GESTURE OF THE ALL SEEING EYE.'

(Crosses his open hands over eyes and then opens them to look directly into the west, turns to the north, hands out, palms upwards.)

'TAKE THE THREAD OF LIGHT MY BROTHER AND COMPLETE THE SACRED CIRCLE.'

(Geb comes and lays his hands on his then returns to the north; all are now facing the altar.)

'THE CIRCLE IS COMPLETE AND ALL IS SAFE.'

(All move slowly to the altar.)

Geb: 'I AM GEB, THAT IS, LORD OF THE EARTH. SON OF HE WHO CREATED ALL THINGS AM I, I SHALL ESTABLISH MY SON OSIRIS AS LORD OF THE

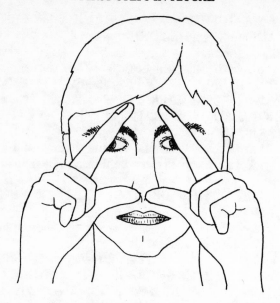

The Gesture of the All-Seeing Eye

EARTH IN MY STEAD. YET IT IS ALSO DECREED THAT HE SHALL BE CAST DOWN BY HIS BROTHER AND SHALL DIE, AND SHALL RISE AGAIN CALLED FORTH BY LOVE. THOU ART OF MY BLOOD AND MY LIFE FLOWS IN THEE, MY LINE IS IN THY SEED AND WE ARE ONE. EAT OF THE BREAD AND THE SALT THAT IS MY BODY AND MY SWEAT AND THUS I SHALL CLAIM THEE.'
(Places small piece of salted bread in the mouth of Osiris. Turns to Horus.)

'SON OF MY SON ART THOU AND LORD OF VENGEANCE, MIGHTY IS THY SWORD AND THE ARM THAT WIELDS IT. THOU ART OF MY BLOOD AND MY LIFE FLOWS IN THEE, MY LINE IS IN THY SEED AND WE ARE ONE. EAT OF THE BREAD AND SALT THAT IS MY BODY AND MY SWEAT AND THUS I SHALL CLAIM THEE.'
(Places piece of salted bread in the mouth of Horus and turns to Anubis.)

'SON OF MY SON ART THOU AND THE WALKER IN THE TWO WORLDS. THOU ART THE GUIDE

AND THE WEIGHER OF HEARTS BEFORE OSIRIS. THOU ART MY BLOOD AND MY LIFE FLOWS IN THEE. MY LINE IS IN THY SEED AND WE ARE ONE. EAT OF THE BREAD AND SALT THAT IS MY BODY AND MY SWEAT AND THUS I SHALL CLAIM THEE.'

(Places piece of salted bread in the mouth of Anubis.)

Osiris: 'I AM OSIRIS SON OF GEB, LORD OF AMENTI AND THE JUDGE OF SOULS. IN ME ALL MANKIND SHALL KNOW LIFE. I AM THE ETERNAL SEED THAT SPRINGS AFTER THE INUNDATION. SEED, ROOT, AND EAR OF CORN AM I, THE SON OF THE EARTH.'

(Turns to Horus.)

'SON OF MY SISTER ART THOU AND SON OF MY BODY, THOU ART OF MY BLOOD AND MY LIFE FLOWS IN THEE. MY LIFE IS IN THY SEED AND WE ARE ONE. I AM THE CORN, EAT OF THE CORN AND THUS SHALL I CLAIM THEE.'

(Places a few kernels of corn in the mouth of Horus, and turns to Anubis.)

'SON OF MY SISTER ART THOU, AND SON OF MY BODY, THOU ART OF MY BLOOD AND MY LIFE FLOWS IN THEE. MY LIFE IS IN THY SEED AND WE ARE ONE. I AM THE CORN, EAT OF THE CORN AND THUS SHALL I CLAIM THEE.'

(Places kernels in the mouth of Anubis and turns to Geb.)

'FATHER OF OSIRIS I NAME THEE AND LORD OF THE EARTH, FROM THY SEED I WAS CALLED FORTH, AND THY LIFE FLOWS IN ME. THY LIFE IS MY LIFE AND WE ARE ONE. I AM THE CORN, EAT OF THE CORN AND THUS SHALL I ACKNOWLEDGE THEE.'

(Places corn in the mouth of Geb.)

Horus: 'I AM HORUS SON OF ISIS AND OSIRIS, BORN OF THE CHILDREN OF THE GODS. I AM THE EYE OF RA AND THE SLAYER OF THE UNJUST, I AM THE SHIELD OF THE WEAK AND THE HAWK OF THE SUN. I AM THE GOLD OF LOVE AND COURAGE.'

(Turns to Anubis.)

'SON OF MY FATHER ART THOU, SON OF MY MOTHER'S SISTER. THOU ART OF MY BLOOD

AND MY LIFE FLOWS IN THEE. MY LIFE IS IN THY
SEED AND WE ARE ONE. I AM THE GOLD OF THE
SUN, TAKE THE GOLD AND THUS I
ACKNOWLEDGE THEE.'
(Puts coin in hand of Anubis and turns to Geb.)

'FATHER OF MY FATHER ART THOU AND LORD
OF THE EARTH. THOU ART OF MY BLOOD AND
MY LIFE FLOWS IN THEE. MY LIFE COMES FROM
THY SEED AND WE ARE ONE. I AM THE GOLD OF
THE SUN, TAKE THE GOLD AND THUS I
ACKNOWLEDGE THEE.'
(Puts coin into hand of Geb and turns to Osiris.)

'MY FATHER THOU ART, BROTHER OF MY
MOTHER'S SISTER. I AM OF THY BLOOD AND
THY LIFE FLOWS IN ME. MY LIFE COMES FROM
THY SEED AND WE ARE ONE. I AM THE GOLD OF
THE SUN, TAKE THE GOLD AND THUS DO I
ACKNOWLEDGE THEE.'
(Puts coin into hand of Osiris.)

Anubis: 'I AM ANUBIS SON OF NEPHTHYS AND OSIRIS,
THE FRUIT OF THE GREAT RITE OF HATHOR. I
AM THE MOUTHPIECE OF THE GODS AND THE
BRIDGE BETWEEN THE WORLDS. I GUIDE THE
SOULS OF THE DEAD TO AMENIT.'
(Turns to Geb.)

'FATHER OF MY FATHER ART THOU, LORD OF
THE EARTH, THOU ART OF MY BLOOD AND THY
LIFE FLOWS IN ME. MY LIFE COMES FROM THY
SEED AND WE ARE ONE. I AM THE KEEPER OF
THE WINE OF REBIRTH. TAKE THE WINE AND
THUS DO I HONOUR THEE.'
(Offers wine to Geb and turns to Osiris.)

'MY FATHER ART THOU, AND FATHER OF MY
BROTHER, I AM OF THY BLOOD AND THY LIFE
FLOWS IN ME. MY LIFE COMES FROM THY SEED
AND WE ARE ONE. I AM THE KEEPER OF THE
WINE OF REBIRTH. TAKE THE WINE AND THUS
DO I HONOUR THEE.'
(Offers wine to Osiris and turns to Horus.)

'SON OF MY FATHER ART THOU, AND SON OF
MY FATHER'S SISTER. THOU ART OF MY BLOOD
AND MY LIFE FLOWS IN THEE. MY LIFE COMES

FROM THY SEED AND WE ARE ONE. I AM THE KEEPER OF THE WINE OF REBIRTH. TAKE THE WINE AND THUS DO I HONOUR THEE.'
(Offers wine to Horus.)

Geb: 'THUS ARE WE BOUND TOGETHER, FATHER AND SON, BROTHER AND BROTHER, BY BLOOD AND SEED, BY BREAD AND SALT AND WINE, BY CORN AND GOLD AND BY LOVE AND POWER.'

Osiris: 'WHAT BINDS THE GODS CAN ALSO BIND MANKIND, AND BY THIS RITE I NAME YOU ALL AS BROTHER AND BLOOD KIN TO ME.'

Horus: 'HERE IN THIS SACRED PLACE WHERE EARTH AND HEAVEN MEET I LAY MY HAND UPON THE ALTAR AND NAME YOU ALL, HEART KIN TO ME.'

Anubis: 'HERE BETWEEN THE WORLDS WHERE TIME HAS NO FOOTHOLD, AND ETERNITY STANDS SILENT LOST IN THOUGHT, I CALL TO THEE ACROSS THE WINDS OF SPACE AND NAME YOU ALL, SOUL KIN TO ME.'

Geb: 'JOIN WITH ME AND FORM THE WHEEL OF LIFE.'
(Holds out hands and grasps left wrist with right hand. Osiris holds out hands and grasps left wrist with right hand, others follow suit, then each man grasps the right wrist of the man next to him thus forging a living chain above the altar.)

Osiris: 'BEHOLD THE LINK OF BROTHERHOOD.'

Horus: 'WHO WOUNDS MY BROTHER DRAWS BLOOD FROM ME.'

Anubis: 'WHO HELPS MY BROTHER I AM BEHOLDEN TO HIM.'

Geb: 'BEHOLD THE STRENGTH OF BROTHERHOOD.'
(They loose hands, Geb turns to face north.)

Geb: 'THE NORTH IS THE PLACE OF GREATEST POWER. I CLOSE THIS PLACE BY MY WILL AND WITH THE GESTURE OF POWER.'
(Repeats gesture as at the beginning and turns to face Anubis with hands out.)
'TAKE THE THREAD OF LIGHT BROTHER AND CLOSE THE WEST.'
(Anubis comes and lays his hands on his, then turns and goes to face west.)

Anubis: 'THE WEST IS THE PLACE OF DEATH AND DREAMS AND THE ULTIMATE TRUTH. I CLOSE

THIS PLACE BY MY WILL AND WITH THE
GESTURE OF THE ALL-SEEING EYE.'
(Repeats gesture as at beginning, turns to face Horus and
holds out hands.)
    'TAKE THE THREAD OF LIGHT BROTHER AND
CLOSE THE SOUTH.'
(Horus comes and lays his hands on his, then turns and goes
to face south.)

Horus: 'THE SOUTH IS THE PLACE OF THE SUN AT NOON
AND OF COURAGE AND LOYALTY. I CLOSE THIS
PLACE BY MY WILL AND WITH THE GESTURE OF
BROTHERHOOD.'
(Repeats gesture as at the beginning, turns to face Osiris and
holds out his hands.)
    'TAKE THE THREAD OF LIGHT BROTHER AND
CLOSE THE EAST.'
(Osiris comes and lays his hands on his and turns and goes
to face east.)

Osiris: 'THE EAST IS THE PLACE OF THE DAWN AND OF
ETERNAL LIFE. I CLOSE THIS PLACE BY MY WILL
AND WITH THE GESTURE OF THE SUN ARISING.'
(Repeats gesture as at beginning then turns to face Geb.)
    'TAKE THE THREAD OF LIGHT BROTHER AND
END THE CIRCLE.'
(Geb comes and lays his hands on his. Then all four come
to altar and stand for a few minutes in silence; they release
the godforms they have assumed and bless them.)

(South)   'IT IS DONE AS IT WAS PLANNED.'
(West)   'AS IT WAS PLANNED SO IT WILL PROCEED.'
(North)   'AS IT PROCEEDS SO IT WILL GROW.'
(East)   'AS IT GROWS SO IT WILL BEAR FRUIT.'
(All)   'AS THE GODS SHALL WILL, SO IT SHALL BE
DONE. THE RITE IS ENDED, THE TEMPLE
CLOSED.'

MAKING EGYPTIAN COLLARS

Materials
White felt, white vilene, or stiff muslin. Cut according to the pattern

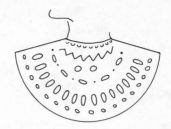

CUT ON LINES

DECORATE WTH BUTTONS, BEADS & SEQUINS

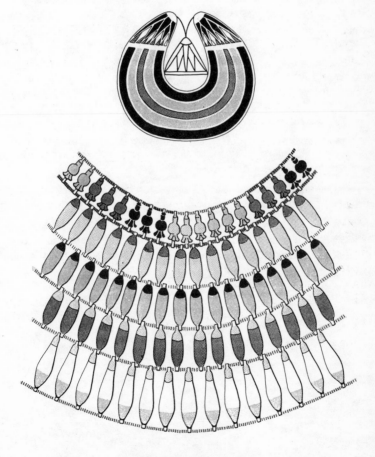

Detail of Egyptian Collar

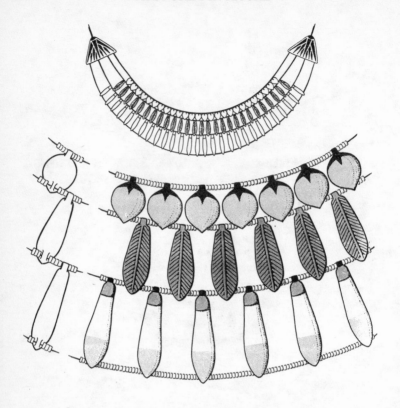

Enlarged Detail of Collar

below and sew tapes or press-studs to the back of the opening. Sew or stick on decorative buttons, sequins and coloured stones to your own pattern, or alternatively you can copy the pattern as given.

4. THE ORPHIC TRADITION

RITUAL ONE: A DIONYSIAN RITUAL

With a few exceptions, the rituals of the Orphic style are full of the joy of living, and are mostly expressed in a combination of dance, song, music and companionship. The whole self participates; subconscious, conscious and superconscious selves becoming intermingled and taking part not only among themselves, but joining with other 'selves' as well. This can bring out a completeness of identity unlike anything you may encounter in other traditions.

However, before we go any further, you can put out of your mind any idea that these Mysteries were a series of drunken orgies. It is true that in later times they degenerated as the old truths were lost, but in the beginning the aim was to achieve an identity with the Godhead. This was seen as a state of Being in which all present at such rites shared with each other, when everyone became part of everyone else, and part of the overall Divinity as well. Wine, the sacred juice of the Sacred Vine, is used in all forms of communion and in many faiths, but in the Orphic Tradition it is the central part of the rite, symbolizing the Divine Son Dionysius.

The vine has been venerated since early times. Its fruit, a basic ingredient of the drink used to bring man and god together, has been used in ritual since the beginning of any form of organized worship. Symbolically speaking, it shows in its shape the divine plan in action — many individual parts forming a living whole. Unlike the apple, another sacred fruit, where each piece of fruit is separate unto itself, every grape is linked to its fellow, apart and yet together, each group forming part of the parent vine, just as each man is linked to his fellow and part of the Godhead. Cut down to the ground in winter, in spring the vine leaps up again as fruitful as ever, the perfect symbol of the sacrificial death and rebirth of the Son of God, in whatever form you may think of Him.

Wine also loosens the etheric part of man, making it easier for the conscious mind to become aware of its ability to contact its higher and lower parts. With the help of the vine, man is able to see himself as part of the cosmic whole, one and indivisible. Long ago, when man first began to lose his ability to see and speak with the spiritual levels, wine helped to lessen the widening gap. Wine taken at certain points during a ritual, combined with the effects of anticipation and physical contact with one's co-workers, can shift the levels of perception to an amazing degree.

The practice of dancing in close circles was another feature of the Orphic Tradition. Those taking part in the rites became aware of the body and all its senses; the feel of the earth beneath their bare feet, the cool air on their bodies — clothed or unclothed — the smell of the flowers and herbs used as wreaths, the taste of the wine and fruit, the sound of evocative pipes and other instruments, and perhaps above all the effect on the vision of a lively circular dance movement continued until the earth and sky seemed to become one. This visual disorientation, combined with all the other stimuli, brought about a state of mind in which it was very easy to achieve alternative levels of perception, and become consciously a part of the Universe. Shared emotion meant a shared sense of brotherhood glorious in its effect.

Gradually, however, the Orphic Tradition degenerated, and the use of wine — first intended as a gentle lift towards the gods — became a self-indulgent vice, destroying the effect it was meant to have and opening doors to the lowest part of the self instead of the highest — although ancient man had not yet built up the remarkable store of unlikely creatures that haunt the subconscious of his modern counterpart. Eventually, the early Church Fathers made a case against the use of music and dancing, although they kept the use of the wine.

There was much more to the Orphic Way, but for the moment we will touch only on the aspect of developing a closeness with nature and the friends with whom you intend to do the ritual. It is meant to enhance a feeling of closeness within a group, spreading through the group mind and strengthening not only the human contacts, but those with the Earth Mother as well. It can be particularly effective if the group is composed of a mixture of races and faiths, for it stimulates the underlying unity of man. Used as a follow-up to an initiation ceremony, it helps complete the integration of a newcomer into the group and into the Group Mind. On a higher level, and with a special intention made beforehand, it can be used to merge the Group Mind of a group or order with an archetypal symbol or an Angelic being, or even with the Elemental Kingdoms, although I would discourage this latter until you (or the group) have had plenty of practice. The denizens of those strange lands can be somewhat capricious and there are many pitfalls for the unwary. The word 'elemental' does not mean only those creatures of the four quarters but covers a whole host of others too — some of which take delight in causing trouble!

The effect of the ritual given here turns on a limited amount of wine and the physical energy and emotion generated by dance movement. This should be a series of rhythmic steps around a central pivot. It is essential that any dance used in this type of working should be circular. There should be a central point — a fire if possible; if not, a simple altar will do. This could be a large stone in its natural setting, or even a cloth on the ground spread with wine, fruit and flowers.

St Ambrose said, 'Just as he who dances in the body . . . acquires the right to share in the round dance, so he who dances in the spirit acquires the right to dance in the round of creation'. During the sacred dances of the Mysteries, man becomes aware of his own divinity, and equates himself with God as he dances the Universe into being. The Dervish and the Hindu have known of this for centuries, and both sects use it in the practice of their faith. In dance, man can go a long way toward unravelling the greatest mystery of them all — himself.

This is primarily an outdoor ritual, suitable for spring, summer or early autumn. At a pinch it can be done indoors, but only if you have lots of room and friendly neighbours. Traditional festival dates, like Guy Fawkes Night, Beltane, Lammas, or Thanksgiving, are good times to do this ritual. Beach parties, and particularly barbeques, provide ideal cover. However, do remember with the latter (particularly in the UK) that you may have to obtain permission from the Local Authority to build a fire either on the beach or common land. If and when such permission is granted, you should also remember that fire can very easily get out of hand, so take extra care and have a blanket or bucket of sand near at hand. Take a plastic bag with you, too, and leave the place neat and tidy when you go. To leave a place of ritual dirty, untidy, and covered with litter, is to destroy all the good you may have done with the ritual itself.

As to time, a weekend is best, preferably sometime during the early evening. Look on this rite with the same enthusiasm you would bring to a birthday or Christmas party. A short fast of about eight hours leading up to the Feast is a good idea; it makes the mind clearer. Food is important. It should consist of wheat cakes, homemade bread, cheese, honey, and fruit, but no meat. The fruit used should be that native to the country, not brought in from abroad. Flowers can be worn, or simply spread around as a decoration, but try to include some vine leaves and some ivy. For the wine, choose something light and not too sophisticated. If you prefer it, you can use pure grape juice. Red wine is preferable to white, as the former is a type derived from the original red wine of ancient times. *Do not bring too much wine* — this is a rite, not an orgy! Enough for about three cups each is quite sufficient.

If you are sure you will not be interrupted, light robes can be worn, otherwise wear fresh clothes, newly laundered. Music is essential. If you have someone who can play either guitar or flute (or both) then you are lucky — use their talents. If not,the god will not mind a cassette! Choose music that is not too modern. Old folk tunes are easier to dance to in this context. Some of the old Greek music is ideal, or the Israeli, as both have a good rhythm for your purpose — quick and light. Do not choose an African beat, or modern disco music: the tradition on which they are based is totally wrong for this type of ritual. You will get a very different influence coming into the rite if you are unwise enough to try either.

One of the nicest things about this ritual is that it is so old it is almost modern. In an age when people get together to sing, dance, and eat, the underlying intention of the whole rite can — and almost always does — pass unnoticed by outsiders. A group of young people with their guitars and a picnic hamper is a familiar sight and causes no adverse comment. Please remember, however, that this is something private and, in its own way, holy. Do not draw attention to yourselves, or give out time and place to all and sundry. The leader of the group should arrive first, so as to be able to greet the others as they arrive and accept their offerings of food, etc. If used, incense should be thrown on the fire; failing that, try to burn pine branches. In the UK and USA suitable incenses can be made up by suppliers. Please, *no* joss sticks — you want to call up Dryads, not Dakinis or Apsaras!

When everyone is ready, you should sit down in a circle around your central pivot, be it fire or altar, man and woman alternately if possible. Start with a short meditation of a few minutes — a young vine in full leaf as a symbol of the group is a good subject for meditation in this instance. The leader should then rise, and fill a large cup or chalice with wine. This he should raise to the east in salute, saying:

'ALL JOY BE TO HIM WHO IS THE GREAT VINE, AND TO THE CHILDREN OF THAT VINE.'

He should then spill some of the wine onto the ground, and move around the circle, letting each person drink from the cup, and exchanging with them the kiss of brotherhood. When this is done, the Feast may begin.

You must remember that this is not just a party with food and drink. It is a rite, a form of communion between each one of you and the God

The Children of the Vine

within, who stands ready to share Himself with all. The talk should be of the group, its aims, ideals, and future plans. Do not spoil the atmosphere with swearing or coarseness. This does not mean that you should all emulate a Sunday School outing; working with the god Dionysius there is bound to be a little ribaldry, but do not let it get out of hand. This is where the strength of the leader must be shown. For him, it is a test of his ability to govern those about him without force, but with firmness. It is a good idea for some of the group to act out a mime based on one of the Greek myths, or even for one of you to read the story aloud. (A warning here: it may not seem like a ritual at this point. Let me assure you that it is — very much so!)

Remember too that where a group gets together, there also will be its Group Mind. You should always, therefore, count one extra as being of the party, the extra being the Group Mind. Many of you will know of customs, particularly in East European regions, concerning the 'unseen guest'. This is no fairy tale. Wherever a group gathers, and the gathering has a purpose to which all its members are committed, be it for a special meal or a ritual, there will also be the extra guest, the Group Mind. Acknowledge this, and give it welcome; honour it with a drop of wine spilt on the ground.

Take your time over this part of the rite; it is all part of the build-up. When he judges the time to be right, the leader should again rise and signal the music to begin. The men should then make a circle facing the fire, and the women an outer circle facing away from the fire. You now have two circles, one male and one female, one moving clockwise, the other anti-clockwise. This produces a double circle of alternating polarities rather like a DNA helix. An alternative to this is one big circle of man, woman, man, woman. If the group is big enough, make two lots of double circles, or two big ones. As you move around, use a short springing step, not a skip, but something more akin to the old Greek dance movements. The same kind of thing can be found in some of the steps used by the American Indians in their rituals.

With the dance goes a chant in a question and answer mode. It is this chant that provides the final push to the whole thing — music, dance and chant. The chant goes like this:

Women: 'WHO IS THE GOD?'
Men: 'WINE IS THE GOD.'
Women: 'GOD IS IN MAN.'
Men: 'MAN IS IN GOD.'
Women: 'WHERE IS THE GOD?'

Men: 'THE GOD IS IN US.'
All: 'DIONYSIUS.'

Repeat this several times, keeping to the beat at all times. Then, still chanting, the leader should break this circle of men and lead the way out, away from the central pivot point. As the last man follows the woman nearest to him should catch his hand as he passes, and lead the women to follow the line. Then the leader should dance into a maze pattern, with everyone still following. When he reaches the centre, he should dance out again, leading the line away to another spot, where the whole thing is repeated. When the second maze is complete, everyone should turn, and the last woman then becomes the new leader and repeats the same maze pattern, but anti-clockwise. This can be kept going until exhaustion sets in, and you feel you can dance no more. Then you should fling yourselves down to rest, letting the laughter and the atmosphere soak into you. If you have enough time, strength and energy, you can start all over again from the chant . . . it will depend on you. However, do not let it go on too long, certainly not into the small hours. Counting the setting-out of the Feast, eating it, etc., plus the chant and the dancing, you should allow for about two and a half hours. When you add to that time to calm down and have a last cup of wine, it will be time to go.

As with all of the rituals in this book, this is an adaption rather than the authentic ritual. Authentic Orphic rituals require a knowledge of ancient dances in the Classical style, and can be very complicated. You may, of course, adapt any or all of this rite to your needs. It is a very comfortable one, and needs little or no depth of training to achieve good results. All rituals have an effect that is over and above the primary intention, and you can therefore expect to be a little tense for about 12 to 24 hours after a high-level ritual, eight hours or so for one less deep. This is normal and need not bother you. If anything does appear to go wrong, above all *do not panic*. 99 times out of 100 it will just be a question of a bad seal on the place or Temple, in which case you have only to go back, open up, and then reseal it tightly for all to right itself.

Although it may seem to be mostly for the under-25s, this ritual is for all ages. Do not think that once you reach 40 it is all over! There are rituals you can undertake and enjoy at any age; it simply does not matter. Intention is all in the art of ritual magic.

RITUAL TWO: FEMALE HEALING RITUAL

Asclepius was the son of Apollo, the Sun God of Ancient Greece; and
as Apollo was also the God of healing it was befitting that his son also
became a healer. His Temple at Epidauros is still a place of pilgrimage
thousands of years after the last priest closed the gates and left it to
the silence and the bees. Of all the ancient sites of that sun-drenched
land, it is perhaps the one with the most atmosphere. The Acropolis,
Delphi, Mycenae and Corinth have been commercialized until there
is nothing left of the sacred. But although Epidauros is, like the others,
a tourist attraction, somehow it still holds a vestige of its greatness,
especially in the late afternoon when the crowds have gone. Then it
is easy to drowse in the sun and see it as it once was, full of people,
but with an air of deep purpose.

Perhaps this was because of its power as a centre of healing and the
dedication that always goes with that work; perhaps it still holds a little
of the Apollonian gift of health and insight. The great theatre, one of
the finest still surviving, is still used to present the plays of Euripides
and Aristophanes during the summer months. The incredible acoustics
enable the faintest whisper to be heard at the back of the rising tiers
of seats. But when the tourists have gone, when the sun is less fierce
and overwhelming, then you may see with the far sight, as I have seen,
the theatre being used as it was intended: the sick laid on pallets where
the actors now stand, and row upon row of white-robed priests and
priestesses focusing their trained minds and healing powers upon them;
using sound, they would chant high and low, now softly, now with
increasing power, then dying away once more into the gathering thyme-
scented dusk. You see, the acoustics work both ways — sound moves
from the stage to the audience, but also from those seated to those below.
The healing power of sound was drawn down to the sick and weary,
channelled by the marvellous architecture of the Temple. It is a power
we are only just beginning to use again in medicine.

Healing is one of the main uses of magic, and the powers of Asclepius
and his Divine Father are still available to us. Even a beginner can heal
if the will and the love is there. The following ritual does not use sound,
because that has to be taught and practised, but it does follow the
Asclepian line and invokes the power of his twin daughters, Hygeia
and Panacea.

One of the greatest needs for healing, and one that is seldom treated
in the right way, is the aftermath of rape. The womb is the sacred centre
of a woman, and its violation is as great a desecration as that of a church.
A church, temple, or any sacred place of worship is a womb wherein

mankind comes to be renewed and made clean and whole. We refer to 'Mother Church' and the words 'She' and 'Her'. The new-born child and adult are baptized in Her, and the great Mysteries of marriage and the celebration of death (and it *is* a celebration) take place within the womb of the church. If blood is spilt within that sacred space it is desecrated and there is an outcry. If a man broke in and masturbated on the altar where the sacred Communion between mankind and God takes place, he would be condemned; it would be labelled as an outrage and offers of help would flood in from all sides.

But when a woman is raped, when the sacred centre where life itself is engendered, of which a man says in the marriage service, 'with my body I thee worship', when that is entered, torn, savaged and left dirty and unclean, what is offered to the woman? She may, if she is lucky, get counselling; relatives and friends, husbands, mothers may gather close and offer love and understanding, but where can she go to be made whole and clean again? *Can* she be made whole and clean again? Yes, she can, with the help of loving and understanding women and by the use of ritual, she — and that sacred place within her — can be re-consecrated and her spirit made whole. It can be done, it has been done. The way is given below. But first an explanation.

There is a tendency when one speaks of laying a woman upon an altar for the inexperienced and the misinformed to scream, 'Black Magic' at the top of their voices. But all things destined to be used for the celebration of the Mysteries, Christian or Pagan, are consecrated upon an altar. Is a woman and the holy place within her less worthy?

Many people reading this book will know how to spiritually cleanse a Temple or room and make it sacred for a ritual. If not, here is a simple version to help you. You will need privacy and quiet, and six or seven women who are willing to put their hearts and souls into the ritual. To cleanse and prepare the room you will need salt and water, a half teaspoon of salt, and a glass of water. Cleanse the water first. Place your open hand over the glass and say;

'CREATURE OF EARTH, BY THE POWER THAT RULES THEE, I CAST OUT FROM THEE ALL THAT IS EVIL AND UNCLEAN. BLESSED BE THOU IN THY CLEANLINESS.' Now place your hand over the salt in the same way.

'CREATURE OF EARTH, BY THE POWER THAT RULES THEE, I CAST OUT FROM THEE ALL THAT IS EVIL AND UNCLEAN. BLESSED BE THOU IN THEY CLEANLINESS.' Tip the salt into the water and circle the room, Temple, or place of working, sprinkling the mixture as you go. This will cleanse the room.

You will need a couch or a table long enough to take the full length of the woman to be healed; cover it with a white cloth. Have a small table, also covered with a white cloth, some three feet in front of it to act as an altar; on it, place containers of salt, water, and sweet oil, some burning incense, and a chalice a quarter full of wine. You will also require a bowl of mixed water and wine and two clean cloths. Two women act as sponsors, the others as witnesses. The woman herself should be dressed in a robe or loose garment, her feet bare, and she and her sponsors stand outside the circle or sacred place. Inside are the other women and the priestess. (A priest may do this ritual, but *only* if the women agree and have complete trust in him as a man.)

The priestess asks the sponsors:

'WHO WILL SPONSOR THIS WOMAN TO BE HEALED?' They must answer and come forward. They take the bowl of water and wine and the cloths. They lay down a cloth for her to stand on and then wash the woman's hands and feet with wine and water, and dry them with the other cloth.

The priestess asks the woman:

'IS IT YOUR WILL AND YOUR DESIRE TO BE HEALED AND MADE WHOLE?'

The woman replies:

'IT IS MY WILL AND DESIRE.'

The priestess instructs the sponsors:

'BRING HER TO THE ALTAR AND LAY HER DOWN.' The sponsors lift the woman over the circle and carry her to the altar and lay her down on it. Thus her cleansed feet never touch the earth. The two sponsors stand at her head and feet supporting them gently so that she is symbolically suspended between heaven and earth.

The priestess faces East, arms outstretched, and says:

'APOLLO, LORD OF THE HEALING HAND, SUN CHILD, VICTOR OF DELPHI, I CALL THEE TO THE EAST IN THE FORM OF THE RISING SUN. WE HAVE NEED OF THEE.' She faces south:

'ASCLEPIUS, SON OF THE SUN, GUARDIAN OF THE SOLAR SERPENT, I CALL THEE TO THE SOUTH IN THE FORM OF THE SUN AT NOON. WE HAVE NEED OF THEE.' She faces west:

'HYGEIA, PRIESTESS OF THE TEMPLE OF THE BODY, I CALL THEE TO THE WEST IN THE FORM OF THE WATERS OF LIFE AND ENERGY.' She faces north:

'PANACEA, PRIESTESS OF THE TEMPLE OF THE QUIET MIND, I CALL THEE TO THE NORTH IN THE FORM OF THE

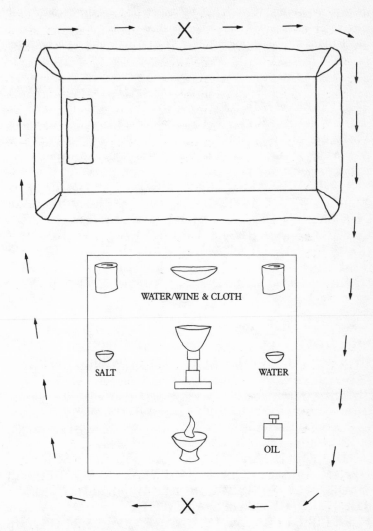

WATER/WINE & CLOTH

SALT

WATER

OIL

DOVE OF INNER PEACE.'
The priestess takes up the incense and goes round to stand over the
woman (see plan), and passes the burning incense up and down her
body.

'WITH BURNING HERBS I CLEANSE THEE, WITH SWEET
SMELLING INCENSE I DRIVE PAIN AND HURT FROM
THEE, WITH SCENTED SMOKE I HALLOW THEE.'
The priestess returns to the altar. (Always move sunwise, making a circle
each time; do not double back.) She takes up the salt and water, cleanses

them as before, and tips salt into the water. (If you can get water from a holy well such as Walsingham or Chalice Well, or from Lourdes, so much the better.) The priestess then takes the salt and water and goes as before to stand by the woman and, tipping the liquid in small quantities into her hand, bathes the face and sprinkles the body and feet.

'WITH SWEET WATER I CLEANSE THEE AND WASH AWAY THE TEARS OF PAIN AND SORROW. WITH SALT I CLEANSE THEE AND MAKE THEE PURE AND SACRED ONCE MORE.' Having said this, the priestess returns to the altar, takes up the chalice, goes to the woman and moistens her lips with wine. Then she lifts the chalice up and invokes the Great Female Principle of the Universe:

'THOU WHO ARE EVER CHASTE AND VIRGIN, THE MOTHER OF ALL LIVING, RENEW AND RECONSECRATE THE SACRED CENTRE OF THIS WOMAN. MAKE HER CLEAN AND CHASTE ONCE MORE. MAKE HER CONSCIOUS OF HER WOMANHOOD AS SOMETHING OF BEAUTY AND HOLINESS. RETURN TO HER, HER IMAGE OF HERSELF, AS A CHILD, MAID, WOMAN AND WISE ONE.' As she speaks she brings the chalice down slowly until it rests upon the womb.

'WHAT IS FILLED WITH LIGHT ABOVE SHALL BE FILLED WITH LIGHT BELOW. WHAT IS PERFECT IN THE UPPER REALMS SHALL BE MADE PERFECT IN THE LOWER.' The priestess then takes the chalice, returns to the altar and picks up the oil, goes to stand by the woman, and makes circles with the oil on her forehead, between her breasts, over her womb, on her palms, and under her feet. As each place is marked she says:

'MADE HOLY ARE THY THOUGHTS AND ALL THY DREAMS, MADE HOLY IS THE HEART WITHIN THEE, MADE HOLY IS THY WOMB. THY HANDS SHALL HEAL THE HURTS OF OTHERS, AND THY FEET SHALL WALK FOREVER IN THE LIGHT.' The priestess returns the oil to the altar and bids the sponsors to help the woman to rise up and stand upon her own feet, unaided and whole. She gives the woman the chalice so she may drink the rest of the wine. The priestess then declares:

'YE WHO ARE PRESENT, BEHOLD YOUR SISTER, RENEWED IN BODY, SOUL AND HEART.' To the woman, she says:

'NEVER DOUBT THAT YOU ARE NOW CLEANSED AND MADE WHOLE AND HOLY. GO OUT INTO THE WORLD

AGAIN AND WALK WITH PRIDE IN YOUR WOMANHOOD.'
Everybody then responds:
'SO MOTE IT BE THIS DAY.'
A small gift of flowers to the woman from her sponsors and witnesses
will make a good ending to the ritual. The wine and water from the
bowl should be given to the earth, and the cloths washed as soon as
possible. The woman should sleep early on that night and eat sparingly
for the next 24 hours.

If, and it is a big *IF*, there is a man either in the family or who is
known to the priestess and acceptable to the women, a further part
to the ritual may be added. However, I emphasize that the woman may
not be able to accept the suggestion and, if so, she should not be made
to do so. A lot will also depend on the ability of the man to handle
the whole thing with delicacy and tact.

At the end of the ritual, the woman is asked by the priestess if she
feels ready to forgive the man responsible. If she says no, then let it
be. If she says yes, then the following may be added to the rite:
One of the sponsors goes to bring the man, who stands as a symbol
for the Male Principle. He is brought to the altar before the woman
and kneels. He takes her hands in his and speaks:
'THOU ART WOMAN, THOU ART HOLY, THOU ART THE
CHALICE. FOR WHAT WAS DONE TO THEE BY MAN, I, AS
MAN SYMBOLIC, ASK THY FORGIVENESS. I OFFER TO
THEE THE HAND OF MAN IN LOVE, IN FRIENDSHIP, AND
IN RESPECT. WILL YOU, AS WOMAN BETRAYED, ACCEPT
ME AS YOUR FRIEND?'
The woman responds:
'I WILL ACCEPT THEE.'
The man then says:
'LET THERE BE PEACE AND LOVE BETWEEN US AND
IN TOKEN OF THIS I OFFER THE KISS OF PEACE.'
He rises and kisses her hands and her brow.
'THOU ART WOMAN, THOU ART BLESSED, THOU ART
MADE SACRED BY THIS RITE. AS MAN SYMBOLIC, I
ACKNOWLEDGE THIS. GIVE ME, I PRAY THEE, THY LEAVE
TO DEPART IN PEACE.'
The woman says to the man:
'DEPART, AND PEACE BE BETWEEN THEE AND ME.'
The man leaves, and the ritual ends in the same way as above.

5. THE WOMEN'S MYSTERIES

THE DANCE OF THE GREAT MOTHER

As I promised in an earlier chapter, here is a ritual entirely for women. There is no specified number involved, just the requirement that there be enough to form a ring (or two rings) around a centre group of four priestesses. There is ample evidence of secret and withdrawn Mysteries pertaining only to women throughout the ages. It is only in more modern times that they appear to have gone to ground. Some of their rites, often greatly changed, have surfaced in the practices of neo-pagan and Wiccan groups but, at least in Britain, there are very few all-women groups, although they are beginning to form slowly but surely. In the Ancient World both sexes had their own secrets and rituals; the males had the Isian priesthood and the Mithraic (to which it would appear most of the Roman army belonged at one time or another) and Nordic battle groups, to mention just a few; for the women there were the old and sometimes very dark rites of Samothraki, Astarte, and Tanith, and the warrior priestesses of the lion-headed Sekhmet. There have, of course, been others throughout history, but persecution forced them to leave little information behind for future generations.

It was because of the growing interest of women in their own rites and practices that some years ago I put together a weekend seminar, the Women's Mysteries, in which we alternate magical practice and theory with modern-day problems, fears, and hidden dreams. Each time it is different because I personally learn so much from the women attending the seminar, and so it grows and changes with time. So far, many female groups and women-only conferences have come out of these weekends, and the feeling of joy and freedom that permeates them is something to remember.

The ritual given here is a memory of that feeling of joy, of the delight that all women should be able to feel in their femininity. The grace,

The Mysterious Symbols of Womanhood

beauty, strength and power that lies within every woman of any age
is something to celebrate. This ritual is such a celebration. There is
in America a singer called Charlie Murphy. One of his tracks, 'The
Burning Times', is a perfect circle dance both in music and words for
any female magical group. I do not know if it is available outside the
USA, but if you can get it, do use it.*

'The Dance of the Great Mother' is a ritual of movement and worship,
so it needs no altar, but it does require that words of the ritual are learned
off by heart. It is basically an outdoor ritual, but it can be worked indoors
if the room is large enough for a circle dance. Every woman has a garland
of flowers and greenery for her hair, preferably made by herself. If you
have long hair, let it down, wear robes of dresses/skirts, it does not matter,
providing it is loose, flowing and feminine and gives you room enough
to move. If it is feasible or safe to go barefoot, then it is a good idea
as it links you to the Earth Mother.

The inner circle is made up of four women; Goddess, Maiden, Wife,
and Wise Woman. Each one wears a garland of a different kind: the
Goddess wears a garland of white flowers and green leaves with a bunch
of white and green ribbons at the back; the Maiden wears a garland
of yellow flowers and green and yellow matching ribbons; the Wife's
garland has pink or red flowers and leaves with the same colour ribbons;
and the Wise Woman has a garland of evergreen leaves and dark red
berries, or black juniper berries only and no ribbons. Apart from this
you will need a besom, a bowl of water with a small bunch of herbs
tied together and floating in it, a chalice of wine, and a wooden bowl
with a mixture of flower petals and leaves, or leaves only if flowers are
scarce, or even pot-pourri. You also require a tape recorder and some
music tapes suitable for dancing.

If you have, or can get, a cauldron, it makes a wonderful centre-piece
for the circle. Fill it with red wine and float petals and berries in it,
and wind leaves and blossom around the rim. The best time for this
ritual is early on a spring or summer evening, at twilight or as dusk
begins to fall. A moon rising is a bonus. The autumn with a fire to
dance around can be just as wonderful but winter can be a little austere,
unless you are in a warmer region such as the West Coast of America
or Australia, where it may be worked at any time of the year.

If you have decided on an outdoor ritual then it is a good idea to
leave your transport in a convenient place and walk the last part of the
way. There is something about walking to a ritual that enhances the

*Catch the Fire, Iceberg Records, 207 East Buffalo Street, Suite 501,
Milwaukee, WI 53202, USA.

whole evening. Food and drink play a big part in the building of the Group Mind. To eat and drink with others is always a binding thing; this is the basis of communion of any kind, and one of the reasons why we instinctively refuse to eat with people we dislike or suspect of dubious behaviour towards us.

Having arrived at your ritual location, the next thing is to make it sacred. If it is possible and you are sure there is no danger, build a fire, even just a small one will add another dimension to the whole event. This should be at one end of the 'dancing floor' — at the other lay out your food, wine, fruit, etc. Try to include only those fruits that are native to the country. Red wines, apple juice, cider but no spirits. Once everything has been arranged the ritual can begin with the clearing of the 'dancing floor'. With the exception of the four aspects of Woman, the rest go aside leaving them a clear space in which to work.

The four group together in the centre, facing inwards. The Maiden holds the water and the bunch of herbs, the Wife has the chalice of wine, the Wise Woman has the besom, and the Goddess has the bowl of leaves and petals. They begin to pace around in a small circle, chanting:

> 'MAIDEN, MOTHER, WOMAN WISE,
> GODDESS WITH THE MOON FILLED EYES,
> SEE THY SERVANTS GATHERED HERE,
> WATCHING, WAITING, WITHOUT FEAR.
> TREAD THE MOON PATH TO THE GLADE,
> GODDESS, MOTHER, PUREST MAID.
>
> HEAR US CALL THEE AS OF OLD,
> MAID OF SILVER, HEART OF GOLD.
> MOTHER MILD WITH SON CHILD FILLED,
> WOMAN WISE IN WISDOM SKILLED.
> GODDESS CLAD IN BEAUTY RARE,
> HOLD US NOW WITHIN THY CARE.'

Maiden: (Moves to the outer perimeter and circles the sacred place sprinkling water with the bunch of herbs.)
'OUT, OUT, ALL THAT IS UNCLEAN AND DEFILED.
OUT, OUT, ALL THAT CANNOT FACE THE LIGHT.
OUT, OUT, FOR HERE COMES THE SILVER FOOTED ONE.'
(She returns to the inner circle.)

Wife: (With the chalice, goes to the outer edge and circles the dancing place, stopping to throw a few drops of wine on the

ground every six steps or so.)
'OUT, OUT, YE DARK ONES OF THE NIGHT.
OUT, OUT, THOU WHO ARE UNBLESSED.
OUT, OUT, LOOK NOT UPON THE MYSTERIES
OF THE MOON GODDESS.'
(She returns to the circle.)

Wise Woman: (Takes the Wife's place at the edge of the circle. She sweeps with the besom out from the centre, sweeping everything away from the dancing floor.)
'OUT, OUT, THOU LOST AND WANDERING ONES.
OUT, OUT, YE DEMONS OF THE UNSEEN WORLD.
OUT, OUT, ALL YE THAT ARE PROFANE.'
(She returns to the inner circle.)

Goddess: (Moves to the outer edge. She circles, sprinkling a few petals and leaves around the circle.)
'BE BLESSED, BE BLESSED, IN HER NAME BE BLESSED AND MADE CLEAN.
BE LOVED, BE LOVED, IN HER NAME BE FULL OF LOVE.
BE WHOLE, BE WHOLE, IN HER NAME BE MADE WHOLE AND PURE.'

The Wise Woman goes to the edge followed by the Maid and Wife, and, with her broom, she sweeps a small part of the charmed circle open. The Goddess remains in the centre. Each woman now enters the circle stepping over the broom to be sprinkled by the Maid, and given a sip of wine by the Wife. Each one then goes to the Goddess and is sprinkled with a few petals and leaves. When all are inside, the Wise Woman closes the gap by laying her broom across it.

Water, wine and flowers are now laid by the food and drink and the four return to the centre and join hands. The other women form a circle around them, or two if there are enough. They begin to circle slowly. If there is a third circle, then one should move in an opposite direction to the others. Move at a walking pace at first, holding hands, then move more quickly, then with a light springing step. From then on go as fast as you like but remember to temper things to the slowest member. Keep to the rhythm of the chant as far as you can.

'SILVER LADY, HEAVEN'S QUEEN, GUARDIAN OF THE WOMAN'S DREAM,

GRANT US STRENGTH WHO WORSHIP THEE,
CHILDREN AT OUR MOTHER'S KNEE.
THOU, OUR HOPE, OUR STRENGTH, OUR NEED, SILVER
CHALICE, SILVER SEED.

'FLOWER MAIDEN, BLESSED SHE, HAIL THOU DARK
PERSEPHONE,
WRAPPED IN SLEEP BENEATH THE EARTH, SHE WAKES
TO BRING US ALL TO BIRTH.
WOMEN CRY AND WOMEN PLEAD, SILVER CHALICE,
SILVER SEED.

'HEAR HER FOOTSTEPS FROM AFAR, ISIS OF THE
SILVER STAR,
SHE FROM WHOM THE SUN IS BORN, GIVER OF THE
RIPENED CORN.
THOU THE PRAYER AND THOU THE CREED, SILVER
CHALICE, SILVER SEED.

'WISDOM'S DAUGHTER, QUEEN TO BE, BINAH OF THE
BITTER SEA,
LEAD US GENTLY TO LIFE'S END, SORROW'S CHILD
AND WOMEN'S FRIEND.
BUT WOMEN BEAR AND WOMEN FEED, SILVER
CHALICE, SILVER SEED.

'CLOTHED IN BEAUTY, FAIR IS SHE, VENUS FROM THE
WINE DARK SEA,
BRINGER OF THE SWEET DESIRE, GODDESS OF THE
INNER FIRE.
MAN BOW DOWN AND GIVE HER HEED, SHE IS THE
CHALICE, THOU THE SEED.'

Repeat the chant if needed.

Rest and get your breath back, then the four go to the food laid out and bless it.

Maid: 'BLESSED BE THE EARTH FROM WHICH THIS CAME, BLESSED BE THOSE WHOSE TOIL BROUGHT IT FORTH, BLESSED BE THOSE WHO EAT OF IT.'

Wife: 'BLESSED BE THIS PLACE WHERE WE EAT TOGETHER, BLESSED BE THE WINE THAT WE SHARE, BLESSED BE WOMAN IN MIND, BODY AND SPIRIT.'

Wise Woman: 'BLESSED BE THAT FROM WHICH WE
                  SPRANG AND TO WHICH WE WILL
                  RETURN, BLESSED BE WOMAN AND MAN
                  TOGETHER, BLESSED BE THE BEGINNING
                  AND THE END.'

Goddess: 'BLESSED BE THIS NIGHT AND THOSE
                  GATHERED HERE, BLESSED BE THOSE IN
                  NEED, SORROW AND PAIN, BLESSED BE
                  ALL LIFE FOR THEY ARE MY CHILDREN.
                  CHILDREN, BLESS ME, FOR WITHOUT
                  YOU I AM NOT.'

All: 'BLESSED BE THE GODDESS, BLESSED BE
                  THE GODDESS, BLESSED, BLESSED,
                  BLESSED.'

Now all may come and be served with food and wine, but the four
may not eat nor drink until the others are served. Then they may break
their fast. Other songs and dances may follow on from here until the
time is judged right to end the evening. Gather up all the food and
anything that is left. Tidy everything up, then reform the circle as before,
with the four in the middle with their broom, bowl, chalice and water.

Maiden: (Facing outwards.)
                  'THE RITE IS ENDED, LET THE EARTH
                  DRINK.'
                  (She pours the water away and puts the bowl down.)

Wife: (Facing outwards.)
                  'THE MOON PREPARES TO DEPART.'
                  (She empties the chalice on the ground and puts it
                  down.)

Wise Woman: (Facing outwards.)
                  'THE MOMENT HAS PASSED, THE GODDESS
                  LEAVES.'
                  (She picks up the broom opening the doorway to the
                  outer world.)

Goddess: (Facing outwards.)
                  'FAREWELL AND FAREWELL, BLESSED BE
                  ALL HERE. I SHALL COME AGAIN.'
                  (She walks from the circle and, if possible, disappears
                  from view. The other three walk round the circle in
                  the opposite direction to that taken in the beginning.
                  Then return to centre.)

Maiden: 'IT IS DONE.'

Wife: 'IT IS ENDED.'
Wise Woman: 'NOTHING ENDS.'
                  (She turns to circle.)
                  'I CHARGE YOU BY THE GODDESS TO KEEP
                  SILENT ABOUT THE MYSTERIES OF WHICH
                  YOU HAVE BEEN A PART THIS NIGHT.'
All: 'SO MOTE IT BE THIS NIGHT.'

All may now say their farewells and the dancing floor cleaned and left sweet and clean. Food may be left for the wild ones, but paper etc. must be taken with you.

6. THE CELTIC TRADITION

FULL MOON RITUAL

The Celtic Path is the natural heritage of the Western Mysteries, partly because the Celts, as a race, infiltrated almost every European country, leaving the stamp of their presence wherever they went. Wherever the love of music, poetry and flowing language is found, there the wandering Celts planted the seed. Wherever a form of the garment known as the kilt is seen, or an instrument based on the use of a pipe and air bag is heard, there too has the Celt passed by.

Celtic Mysteries, like the race itself, are highly complex, with many interconnecting lines of thought and usage. Yet for all that, they remain remarkably fluid and far-reaching, with symbolism both beautiful and very intricate. It can take a lifetime to study the Celtic Tradition fully, but the main forms and archetypes are fairly easy to contact. They are part of the very soil of Britain, and of anyone with even the slightest trace of the blood of Albion. They still wait to be called forth from the depths of the racial mind.

One of the main archetypes of this tradition is that of the Sacred Head. The Celts have always given a lot of attention to this particular magical image. In the Qabalistic tradition, this would equate with Kether, the point of manifestation. The whole of England abounds with place names and allusions to the Sacred Head: Nag's Head, King's Head, Horse's Head, and many, many other variations. The old name for head, *pate*, is a common name for lanes and roads in country places. Thus we have Pate's Hill, Pate's Manor, Royal Pate, and many others. Headless horses, nuns, highwaymen, and coachmen, to say nothing of a few Royal ladies, haunt many of the older roads, houses and churches, and beheading was for many centuries *the* form of death, being, in former times, the means of sacrifice in early rites, and more latterly the form of punishment which overtook those persons convicted of crimes against the state or the monarch. It was long the custom to display the heads of such traitors on poles above Tower Gate in London. The tribe of the Icenii, ruled at one point by the famous Boudicca, were much given to lopping off the odd Roman head, impaling it on a pole, and using it thereafter as a kind of grisly standard with which to go into battle.

Perhaps the greatest of the Head archetypes is that of Bran. Legend tells us that although killed in battle, Bran nevertheless ordered his head to be carried back to his native land. It took a long time getting there, and along the way the head talked and sang and discussed the day's events with its former companions each night when they camped. It is said that at last the miraculous head was buried beneath the White Tower within the Tower of London, there to guard the whole land. While it remains undisturbed, it is said, the land of Albion will remain safe from invaders.

For those interested in pursuing the legends of the Celts, I can recommend a set of books by Evangeline Walton under the collective title of *The Islands of the Mighty*. Here the tales we know as the Mabinogion are told in fictional form without losing any of the beauty of the original version, but which lack the dryness of the more scholarly translation. If one can read Welsh, of course, the original has a charm all its own. Unfortunately, the sheer poetry of the original loses much in translation.

Apart from Bran, there are a bewildering number of other Celtic deities, and the confusion is made worse by the fact that the Celts can be divided into Irish/Scottish Celts, Welsh/Cornish Celts, and Breton Celts, every group having slightly different names for the same gods. The Gallic line adopted many of the Roman gods as well and happily mixed them with their own; but by virtue of living on an island, the Celts of the Blessed Isles, as they are called, kept to a much purer form of worship. This has had the effect of allowing many of their methods and rituals to come down to us in folklore and traditional celebrations comparatively little altered. Many of their old meeting places, for instance, are still held as such; still others over the centuries became a different kind of meeting place and are now the old inns and public houses so beloved of Englishmen. As the old faith died out, these places became simply a place to rest on a long journey. The number of inns called 'The Green Man' is therefore legion, holding, in reality, the memory of Cernunnos, the horned fertility god of the Celts, and indeed, of those who came before them. 'The Nag's Head' or 'Horse's Head' relates to Epona, the horse goddess whose symbols once covered the hills of England and are still visible in one or two places, cut into the chalk. Even today, at the big country fairs that are celebrated annually all over the country, the great shire horses are decked out in strangely wrought brasses, and have their manes and tails braided in the ancient manner of horses going to the sacrifice long ago. Merrie England takes on a new meaning when you realize that the word 'merrie' means 'enchanted' or 'fairylike'.

To do justice to such a vast subject, one needs a book, not just a chapter of a few pages; but this Tradition can be a rich source of pathworkings and rituals if you have a mind to write your own one day, and in that event, the list of books at the end of the book should prove very helpful.

As with all other rituals I have gathered for this book, this one is in the Celtic style rather than being an actual original rite, since all such rites remain the custody of those whose duty it is to guard them. This particular ritual can be worked alone, or with any combination of up to four people, but no more than four. To do it alone requires a certain amount of courage, for it needs an outdoor setting and a moonlit night in a country place. It *must* be as quiet and private as possible. However, a garden would do, if it is not overlooked by other houses. Late spring, summer or early autumn are the best times for its use.

You will need salt, water, four handfuls of corn, a bottle of mead (*not* wine), a chalice from which to drink, two containers for the salt and water, something on which to lie down, and some fairly thick string or rope. If you are sure of privacy wear robes or, best of all, nothing. This is the one ritual where the absence of clothing enhances the whole effect and the eventual outcome. If this is not possible, then bathe (as always) and put on clean clothing. It is a good idea to walk at least part of the way to the chosen site, for there is something about walking through the quietness of the night toward a sacred meeting place that defies all attempts to describe it.

If you decide to work in a pair, then this should comprise of one man and one woman; if in a threesome, two men and one woman, or vice versa; and if in a foursome, then two of each sex. It simply does not work if all the participants are of the same sex. Choose a clear night with as little cloud as possible, and as near to the Full Moon as you conveniently can. The intention is to unite yourself with the Celtic Race Soul, using four of the archetypes to project yourselves toward the fifth.

Obviously, the more Celtic blood you have in you, the more you will react to a Celtic ritual; but even those of a different race should feel an influx of power, owing to the fact that animal totems form part of the prehistory of every race, and through those totems anyone can receive the contact that this rite provides. Again, it is the intention with which one comes to a rite that provides the thrust-block to the rite itself. Anyone can use any tradition, if they will only try to reach that point where all races blend into the single life wave of the planet.

You can now start the ritual process. When the chosen place has been reached, make sure that it is clear of litter and debris. Select a fairly flat piece of ground and with the string make a circle big enough to enclose one person lying down, two people lying foot-to-foot, three people in a 'Y' formation, or four people lying in a cross formation, depending on the number of participants. Once this circle is made, make sure that you have all you need inside it. You do not want to have to break the circle to get something you may have forgotten. Lay out the rug on which you will be lying, and place the chalice filled with mead in the centre of the circle. Now charge the salt and water, as follows: place the thumb and little finger of the right hand together, keeping the three middle fingers straight. Point them at the salt, and say:

'CREATURE OF EARTH, I BLESS THEE. I CALL FORTH FROM THEE ALL EVIL, THAT THOU MAY'ST BE USED TO CLEANSE THIS PLACE OF WORKING. IN THE PRESENCE OF LIGHT, THIS CREATURE OF EARTH IS CHARGED.'

Do the same with water, and then tip the salt into the water, and use the combined elements to sprinkle around the circle you have set out with the string. Now find your compass points, standing in the middle, facing outwards. Whoever is leading the rite should now take the corn, walk to the eastern edge of the circle, and throw a handful of corn just outside it, saying:

'CERNUNNOS OF THE TWELVE TINES, I BID THEE WELCOME. GRANT A BLESSING ON OUR WORK AND KEEP US FROM HARM THIS NIGHT.'

He should then walk to the south, and throw another handful of corn outside the circle, saying:

'EPONA, WHITE MARE OF THE HILLS, I BID THEE WELCOME. GIVE A BLESSING TO OUR WORK AND KEEP US FROM INTERRUPTION DURING THIS NIGHT'S WORK.'

Moving to the west, and after throwing the corn on the ground, he should then say:

'MONA, SACRED COW OF THE SACRED ISLE, I BID THEE WELCOME. BRING A BLESSING TO OUR WORK, AND GUARD US WITHIN THIS CIRCLE.'

Lastly, moving to the north, he should throw the last of the corn, and welcome the last and greatest of the Guardians;

'ARTOR, GREAT BEAR, ARTHUR AND LORD OF LOGRES, I BID THEE WELCOME. PLACE A BLESSING ON OUR

The Four Great Guardians of the Blessed Isles

WORK, AND GRANT US PEACE IN HEART, MIND, AND
BODY THIS NIGHT.'

As each figure is called, it must be visualized as strongly as possible.
When all this has been done, the next phase can start. If one person
alone is working, then he should lie down in the centre of the circle,
extending arms and legs as if filling a five-pointed star, moving the chalice
to a place between the thighs. If two people are working as a pair, then
they should lie foot-to-foot, with the chalice between them. Three people
should take up the 'Y' formation, and put the chalice where everyone's
feet almost touch. For four people the shape is that of an equal-armed
cross, again with the chalice in the middle between everyone's feet.
Only in the case of an individual working alone are the limbs extended.
Otherwise, only the arms are outstretched, and just touching. Take
care not to let any part of the body go outside the circle, not because
it is dangerous, but simply because this spoils the symmetry of the
shape.

When you have arrived at this point, lying in the quietness of a moonlit
night, you should begin to build up the four great Guardians of the
Blessed Isles at the four quarters around you. Above you the fifth hangs
waiting: the Great Cauldron of Ceridwen, the Moon in its fullness.

Lie quiet and calm. Let the sounds and scents of the night seep into
you. Draw the air into your lungs in soft, short intakes, sifting each
scent as it comes and trying to identify it. Listen not only to the night
sounds, but to the silence itself, the most potent sound of all. Let the
earth cradle you, relax into it, and feel the Earth Mother reaching up
from beneath you to hold and comfort you, her children. Feel the grass
and soil under your hands, and know that part of you is made of the
same substance. Watch the Moon as she climbs the hill of the night
sky, and when she reaches her highest point, close your eyes and think
of yourself as part of a wheel, each one of you being a spoke of it. It
will start to spin slowly, as if a giant hand were turning it and you,
but there is no need to feel fear. It is like a cosmic carousel, part of
the Wheel of Life spinning on the soft green turf of England, or the
spirals such as we see cut into the silent Celtic Crosses by unknown
hands long ago.

The wheel that is you will begin to spin faster. You are part of all
that this Island Race has ever been or ever will be, and the wheel that
is you will lift from the earth, carrying the essence of your race upward,
spinning and turning like the Castle of Arianrhod, on and up to the
Great Cauldron that gleams above you, black on the outside, silvery
white on the inside. Closer and closer you will spin, until you are part
of the whiteness itself, blending with it, and looking down on the earth

lying dark green in the light you are shedding upon her.

The sacrifice is made. The race essence has been offered up to the most ancient of the Grails, to be reborn and remade. The countryside lies beneath you, waiting for you to bring the Mystery of the Grail down and spread it like a blessing over the whole land. Far below is a small circle of light in which lie tiny figures. Around it stand four gigantic forms, the Guardians you called forth, seen now in their full stature: a 12-tined stag lifting proud antlers, the Horned One, pawing the ground as it turns its head from side-to-side; a white mare, gleaming in the moonlight, stamping an impatient hoof, head tossing, alert for the stranger's footfall, blowing faint whisps of white breath from her nostrils; a black and white spotted cow, the most ancient of the Guardians, gently cropping the grass as she waits with the patience of her kind, and in the north, the Great Bear, the 'Artor' of our race, swaying as bears do from side to side, guarding those of its kind and blood.

Once more, blend with the whiteness around you, spinning gently, but floating to the earth again, closer and closer until you feel the grass take up your weight once more, relaxing into it and letting it buoy you up. Now lie quietly for a while, and let the sights, sounds and scents return to fill up your body in return for what you brought down with you — the Grail Blessing. Bring your arms slowly and gently to your sides, move your body, and sit up, taking your time and letting everything around you welcome you back. When whoever is leading the rite feels ready, he should stand up, and take up the chalice, move to the east and spill a little mead on the earth, saying:

'CERNUNNOS OF THE TWELVE TINES, WE THANK THEE FOR THY BLESSING, AND THY PROTECTION.'
Then he should go to the south and say:
'WE GIVE THANKS TO THEE EPONA FOR THY BLESSING AND THE GIFT OF QUIETNESS.'
Then, going to the west, he should say:
'MONA OF THE SACRED ISLE, WE THANK THEE FOR THY BLESSING AND THY GUARDING.'
Lastly, he should go to the north and say:
'ARTOR, GREAT BEAR, ARTHUR AND LORD OF LOGRES, WE GIVE THANKS FOR THY BLESSING, AND FOR THE BEAUTY AND PEACE OF THIS OUR LAND.'
Make sure that a drop of the mead has been given to all the Guardians, and then share the rest between you. Share also what you have done with the whole land.

Now you can untie the knot of the string circle and wind it up, moving anti-clockwise and saying:

'AS I WIND THIS CORD, SO LET THE CIRCLE BE CLOSED.'
Gather up your things, and make sure that you have left the place sweet
and clean. You may depart when you have had a hot cup of tea or coffee.

If this ritual is performed regularly, and in the same place, that place
will become set apart on the inner levels, and a holy place in its own
right. You will find that if you persist, a welcoming feeling is extended
to you as you approach the place. The more often they are used, the
more quickly the four figures will build up, and the more powerful
they will become. This will soon start to affect the whole countryside
around. For those concerned with wildlife and ecology, this ritual will
bring a satisfaction and unity with the earth not previously felt. Of all the
rituals in this book, this is my own favourite, and the one which has
given me most in its performing. It touches a level far deeper and higher
than the most elaborate ceremonies can every do — at least for me.
It is perhaps because here we are for once not asking, but bringing.

7. THE SOLO MAGICIAN

RITUAL ONE: THE WARRIOR GUARDIAN

The Blessed Isles in particular have a long tradition of Warrior Guardians. In many ways they are the descendants of the Priest-Kings of Egypt, their function is to gather wisdom, teach it, practise it and guard it. The names of Arthur, Merlin, Cuchulain, Bran, Gwydion, Math, Rob Roy, Robert Bruce and Llew Llaw Gyffes — and Boudicca also — come to mind. Every land well loved is worth defending, and the role of the Warrior Magician should not be lost as so much that is of value has been lost, simply because no one thought to write it down. It is all too easy for traditions and ways to die out when the last holder of the secret dies without passing it on. I am, so my students tell me, paranoid about putting things down and keeping records. My excuse is that so many things have now gone forever because there was no one near to take them on or write them down, and the future will always have need of true records.

Magicians are not always known for their capabilities as warriors, but the warriors are there under the robe and the lamen. To arouse the Mars within can be dangerous, but unless you try you will never know how to control the power. Learning magic is a tricky business, but spell-burnt fingers teach you a lot . . . fast!

This is, as you will have guessed, a solo ritual, and although I have written it for a man it may just as easily be worked by a woman, as a Warrior Priestess. In fact these two rituals are more or less androgynous. You will need in your sacred place an altar, covered with a red cloth, and a spear or a sword and shield if you have one. Wear a dark red robe; if you only have a black one, tie around it a thick dark red girdle (my apologies to my American friends for whom a girdle is *not* necessarily something you tie around a robe!). Bare feet are best if working indoors; if not, wear thick sandals. Indeed, if you live in a flat with neighbours living below, leave this ritual until you can do it out of doors — it can get noisy.

Incense should be of the 'hot' Martian kind, and any reputable occult supplier will be able to furnish a ready-made incense, or provide the raw ingredients for you to blend yourself. Place five red candles on the altar, five being the number of Mars, red the colour of the Warrior; they should be the only light source. A statue, symbol, or picture of a warrior should act as an altar piece and a tape recorder with some martial music is the last requirement. Mars, from Gustav Holst's *The Planets*, some parts of Prokovieff 's *Romeo and Juliet* (mainly the 'fight' scene), and the film music from Olivier's *Henry V* are all good choices. If you can record the music so that it flows from one piece to another without a break it will help the atmosphere to build up. One side of a 90-minute tape will give you enough time for the whole ritual.

Carrying the sword and shield, or the spear, come to stand before the altar, or, if out of doors, the place where you have arranged the ritual implements. Stand quietly holding the weapons for a few minutes, then go to the east and salute it with the sword/spear. In the imagination build up the figure of Arthur Pendragon with Glastonbury Tor behind him. When you have it as clear as possible, salute him with the sword:

'HAIL ARTHUR, KING OF THE ISLES OF THE BLESSED. I AM HERE TO TAKE MY WATCH OVER THE KINGDOM ON THE INNER LEVELS, WITH OTHERS OF MY KIND.'

Move to south; there you build the image of the Saxon King Alfred, who is credited with the formation of the first British navy. Behind him there are the high cliffs of the coast and the sea winds blow his cloak away from his shoulders. Salute him with the sword/spear:

'HAIL ALFRED, LORD OF BRITAIN, I AM HERE TO TAKE UP MY POST AS SENTRY ON THE INNER LEVELS AND TO GUARD THE APPROACHES TO THESE ISLES, WITH MY PEERS.'

Move to the west; and there the image is one of Merlin the Archmage with his staff bearing a carved horse's head. Behind him you see the dark forests of his native Wales. Above his head hovers a falcon. Salute him:

'HAIL MERLIN, ARCHMAGE AND GUARDIAN OF THIS LAND. I AM HERE TO OFFER MY HEART AND HAND ON THE INNER LEVELS TO DEFEND THIS LAND FROM ITS FOES.'

Move to the north and build there the image of Herne the Hunter, horn-crowned and cloaked, astride a black stallion, two wolfhounds at his heels. Salute him:

'HAIL HERNE, ANCIENT DEFENDER OF GRAMMERYE
AGAINST THE LORDS OF THE DARK FACE. I AM HERE TO
OFFER MY SWORD-ARM IN YOUR ETERNAL STRUGGLE
AGAINST THE DARK.'

Return to the altar and turn on the music. As it fills your place of
working let it flow through you and begin to stir your blood. Let your
body sway and your feet begin to move. Soon the music and the
atmosphere within your working place will build up and you will feel
the surge in the blood that lifts the heart of every warrior before he
goes into battle. There are times to be priest and magician, and there
are times to be the magical warrior. Dance now as the ancient defenders
did, shake your sword and stamp your feet, and mime the sword and
spear play as you circle the Temple. You are the Warrior Priest upon
the inner levels and you are ready to defend the Land against any who
would seek to break its defences on the inner levels.

Dance until the music ends then rest, leaning on your sword or spear.
Move with dignity to the east and salute the King; he turns to face the
east and together you take up the vigil of the east from the top of the
ancient Tor. You keep watch with the inner eye, and soon before you
there builds the land to the east of where you stand. Look over it closely
and you will find you are able to see all the way to the coast and to
the sea beyond. You will see its ancient peoples and towns and marvel
at the continuity of its life and laws. Gradually there builds up around
you other figures. First the knights of the Round Table — Lancelot,
Gawain, Kay, Bedevere, and others — then slowly the others, archers
and foot soldiers, grenadiers and Templars, crusaders and Highlanders,
soldiers from every century gathering around you. Always at your side
and a little in front of you is the King, and from time to time he turns
his head and nods to you. When you feel the time is right, salute him,
bow, and go to take up the vigil of the south.

Here Alfred stands high on a cliff overlooking the sea, and you take
your place beside him. You can feel the sea winds tugging at the robe
and hair, taste the salt on your lips. Before you, you see passing, the
ships that have sailed these waters since earliest times, coracles, and
small wooden craft, high-prowed galleons, and men-of-war. From all
centuries they come, still sailing the seas they loved and defended. There
sails the *Golden Hind* with Drake at the prow, Sidney, and Raleigh,
and those who sailed with them. Cook and Cabot are there, as are the
crew and captains of smaller ships that struggled against all odds at
Dunkirk and won. Still their shades patrol the seas and guard the
approaches to the Blessed Isles. When you have fulfilled your time,
salute Alfred, bow, then go to take up the vigil of the west.

Merlin acknowledges your presence and you both turn to the west. Before you is a dark sky jewelled with lightning, and together with Merlin you use your magical strength to keep it from overpowering the land before you. Every land is threatened from time to time by the Dark Ones and in every land there are those who from time immemorial have taken their turn on such vigils. Around you, you see others of your kind; you may even see faces you know who like yourself have offered their service to this task. Some still have physical bodies, others have withdrawn to the inner levels and take their turn in the vigils until such time as they must once again wear a form of flesh and blood. You can feel the energy being demanded of you as you work together to keep the darkness from overwhelming the land. When your time is up, another cloak-wrapped form steps to your side to take your place. You turn and salute Merlin, who raises his staff in answer, you bow, and move to the north.

The stallion snorts and dances sideways as you approach Herne; behind him you can see the shadowy forms of ancient shamans, druids, and older and darker figures that wear strange robes and headresses. Around them move four-footed shapes — wolves, bears, tusked boars, and the white-coated, red-eared Hounds of Annwn. Herne looks down at you and raises his hand in salute, and you answer in kind, one of the shadow figures brings to you a horse with a silver bridle and you mount. The Hunt begins.

Out onto the inner levels of the Isle of Grammerye you sweep and the land rolls away beneath the flying hooves. Around you jostle the ancient magical warriors, and in between them you see glimpses of the Heroes of legend. Later still as you sweep across the mountains and moorlands you are joined by the Shining Ones, the Faery Folk, Aengus Oge and his warriors ride with you, circling the whole of Grammerye, checking and searching and guarding. Sometimes a figure from a nightmare looms out of the twilight and it is set upon by the mighty throng of the Hunt. Sometimes you pause and wait, and another figure will join you, a warrior from earth whose life has been made forfeit and who will be taken by the Hunt to a place of rest. So passes this vigil and all too soon you are back within the enclosure of your sacred place. You dismount and salute Herne, he acknowledges your gift of time and waits for the Temple to be closed. You walk to the altar and lay down your sword and place both hands palms-down upon the altar.

'HAIL TO THEE GUARDIANS OF THIS LAND, STRENGTH TO THEE AND COURAGE ALSO, I GIVE THANKS FOR THE BLESSING OF THY PRESENCE AND FOR THE

CONTINUING WATCH OVER US ALL. I COUNT IT AN HONOUR TO TAKE MY PART IN THIS AND PLEDGE MY SUPPORT TO YOU IN THIS WORK. SO MOTE IT BE.'

Lay the sword upon the altar and go to the east; salute.

'HAIL AND FAREWELL ARTHUR, HIGH KING OF BRITAIN AND GUARDIAN OF ITS LAWS AND DESTINY. IF THERE IS NEED, CALL ME AND I WILL COME AND TAKE MY PLACE BESIDE YOU.'

Move to the south.

'HAIL AND FAREWELL ALFRED, KING OF ENGLAND, GUARDIAN OF THE SEAS. I COUNT MY TIME WITH THEE AN HONOUR, AND PLEDGE MY SUPPORT TO THEE WHEN THERE IS NEED. SO MOTE IT BE.'

Move to the west.

'HAIL AND FAREWELL MERLIN, ARCHMAGE OF BRITAIN, GUARDIAN OF THE INNER LEVELS OF GRAMMERYE. MY PLEDGE TO THEE STANDS, CALL ME AND I WILL COME. SO MOTE IT BE.'

Move to the north.

'HAIL AND FAREWELL HERNE, HUNTER AND DESTROYER OF THE DARK. I WILL RIDE WITH THEE WHEN THOU HAST NEED OF MY PRESENCE. SO MOTE IT BE.'

Return to the altar. Then put out the first red candle.

'RETURN TO THY PLACE ARTHUR KING OF BRITAIN.'

Put out the second candle.

'RETURN TO THY PLACE ALFRED KING OF ENGLAND.'

Put out the third candle.

'RETURN TO THY PLACE MERLIN ARCHMAGE.'

Put out the fourth candle.

'RETURN TO THY PLACE HERNE THE HUNTER OF EVIL.'

Put out the fifth candle.

'THIS SACRED PLACE IS CLOSED AND ALL IS AS PEACE. SO ENDS THIS RITE.'

This ritual can be used by anyone for the guarding of any land — simply replace the four guardians with heroes, kings, godforms of that land. Women can replace them with Elizabeth I, Eleanor of Aquitaine, Dion Fortune, and Boudicca, for example (an interesting gathering if nothing else!). Use your knowledge and research to find your own guardians to work with.

You can also adapt the ritual for a longer vigil. Every magician should be prepared to take an all-night vigil once in each Tide or Season. Then you choose either to watch over one quarter, or to perambulate the coast on the inner levels. Alternatively, you can keep spiritual vigil by the altar, flowing out your energies and love to those in need throughout the night. A vigil such as this is usually made from sunset to sunrise. It does take a lot of stamina and you would be wise to start with a one hour vigil and increase it by one hour each Tide, taking a full two years to work up to the all-night vigil.

RITUAL TWO: THE HEALER PRIESTESS

The same instructions apply to this ritual as to 'The Warrior Guardian'. It can be worked by a man or a woman, although I have written it here for a woman. It is in a shamanic style as this gives a very wide range of use, both in the type of godforms and totems and in the use of locations and methods of drawing down healing power.

It is wrong to think that only certain gifted people have the power to heal; everyone has it to some degree — some more, some less. All loving parents have it for their children when they are hurt or upset, but strangely enough often fail to realize that husband and wife can heal each other because the same love and need to protect is there.

The power of healing is increased by love — if someone you love is in pain, your desire to alleviate that pain becomes a powerful incentive to draw down the power needed to help them. Some people have enough love for everyone, some are able to block out any feeling of dislike and simply heal because that person needs help. But no one is completely altruistic in this world. It is important for a student of magic to realize that the work will not make you a saint! Often pressure of magical work on personality flaws will bring out the worst in people. It is then that they start to tell all and sundry what powerful magicians they are, or that they are the High Priest of a godform. It is as well to remember that such deities choose their priests personally and not vice versa, and do not take kindly to their names being used or their priesthood claimed in a haphazard manner. If your service to a particular godform or tradition is offered and accepted, confirmation will not be slow in coming; until that time, keep your own counsel.

In the true shamanic tradition the link with a totem animal is often found by means of a 'Spirit Journey' which is taken in conjunction with a purification rite and a strict fasting régime. There are many people all over the world who have taken such journeys along those correct lines and under the guidance of real shamans. However, not everyone

The Way Lies Open to Those Who Dare

has the opportunity to do this. They may have commitments to a job or profession, to their families, or it may be financially impossible for them to undertake such training. I do not claim shamanic training for myself beyond what I know through the faculty of far-memory. What is offered here is something along those lines which, if followed strictly, will bring you a totemic link with which to work, and also show you how to increase your healing ability for yourself and others. In addition, it will, for good measure, link you more deeply with the earth and Her other children.

The first task is to purify the body and cleanse it inside and out. Now it is silly to undertake a strict fast if you are travelling to work and undergoing stress and pressure for some 12 hours of every day. The need then, is for a graded fast that will allow you to work and yet will slowly accustom your body to the idea of fasting. The whole thing will take you two full weeks. There is no way to cut corners — it's been tried and it does not work. If you are too impatient to give two weeks to it, then leave it.

Start ahead of time on a Saturday by getting in a supply of bottled pure spring water. If you have a water filter you can use that at home, but you will still need the bottled water for work. First thing Monday morning you must give up tea, coffee, and alcohol, as well as fruit squashes etc. Your only source of liquid will be pure water, at least three bottles a day (for the next two weeks). You will have to watch yourself; your subconscious is not going to do without the things it likes without a struggle. The subconscious can think up the most devious ways of making you forget, so watch out. Water is one of the greatest purifying substances known and, if allowed to do so, will clean out your body toxins quicker than anything else.

It's Wednesday; in addition to tea, coffee, etc, you are going to give up cakes, biscuits, and any form of dessert. You can have fresh fruit, but no tinned fruits. On Friday you cut back again — no cheese and no preserves such as marmalade and jams, though you can have pure honey. Saturday and Sunday have a breakfast and a late dinner, but no lunch. If you normally have your main meal midday, then either breakfast or supper will have to go.

By the time Monday comes round again you continue to have just two meals a day, but cut down on your bread and potatoes (one slice of bread morning and evening and just one potato with your large meal), making them up with fresh vegetables. Wednesday of the second week and it's no meat; you can have fish instead. Oh yes, and no potatoes and no bread either. The second Friday, have water and two pieces of fresh fruit for breakfast, for lunch and for dinner. Take the time to visit a large record shop or occult supply shop and pick up a tape of native drumming or, if you have a drum, record about 30 minutes of drumming on a tape. On Saturday you will have just water all day; in the evening you will be doing the purification rite.

From the Saturday afternoon until Sunday morning try not to talk unless you absolutely have to — come to some arrangement with your family. If possible send them to your mother-in-law or some other member of your family for the weekend. If you feel up to it, go for a walk somewhere where it's green or at least where there are few people. You may feel a little weak, so if you feel there is any danger of you not being able to get back, then simply sit or lie quietly for a few hours.

In the early evening run a warm (not hot) bath and sprinkle two good handfuls of sea salt in it. While it's running make up the bed with a clean bottom sheet. It is a relaxing bath as well as a physically cleansing one, but do not stay in it for very long, no more than 15 minutes. Wash your hair and clean under your nails thoroughly. When you get out take a clean top sheet and wrap it around yourself like a blanket and sit or lie on the bed. If it is cold weather, then use a thick blanket instead of the sheet, but do not heat the room. You are trying to simulate the conditions in which a true shamanic journey would be taken.

You will be feeling rather weak and maybe a little dizzy now from the lack of food, keep some water near you, but sip it slowly when drinking. You may find you will urinate more frequently with nothing to prevent the water going quickly through your system. When you move, do it slowly or you may feel faint. Lie quietly for a while without thinking of anything in particular, but do not let yourself fall asleep — this is important.

You may find there is a feeling of swaying, or the room may feel as if it is moving in a circle; now it is time to start the journey. If you have managed to get a drum tape this is when you should put it on. If not, then simply use your inner ear and your memory, and listen to a drum beat in your head. Vary it; loud and quick, quieter and slow, a broken rhythm of quick and slow taps, and then a steady monotonous beat. At some point you will want to scream and throw tape and recorder out of the window. Don't; force yourself to lie still. Don't *listen* to the drum, let the sound move through you. The sound will begin to take form, gradually building into a living tree that you find yourself climbing, up and up and up.

At some point you will no longer hear the drums and instead you will be enveloped in a world of green leaves and branches. You move aside a branch and find, as if it is the most natural thing in the world, a footpath leading into a forest. Start walking.

Keep your eyes open and your mind alert, and note what you see. Animals and birds, snakes and insects will cross your path; they will take no notice of you — walk on. You come to a pool of clear water which you may drink from, but look carefully at the reflection you see in the water, it may not be a face you recognize. Continue through the forest. You will come to a clearing which is also a sacred burial ground. Raised on platforms all around you are the blanket-wrapped forms of long-dead chiefs. Beneath the platforms are bows and arrows, spears, and beautiful beaded robes. Touch nothing. Go on walking. Ahead of you there is a patch of thorn bushes and in the midst of them you will see an animal or bird of some kind, caught and unable to move. This will be your totem.

Sit down and watch the creature, it will also regard you. Then address it.

'CREATURE OF MY SPIRIT JOURNEY TELL ME YOUR NAME.'

The creature, using a thought voice, will say: '*No I cannot give you my name for that will give you power over me.*'

'UNLESS YOU GIVE ME YOUR NAME I WILL NOT SET YOU FREE AND YOU WILL DIE. IT IS BETTER TO SERVE THAN TO DIE. GIVE ME YOUR NAME AND WE WILL BE FRIENDS.'

'*If I give you my name will you promise never to harm me or my kind?*'

'I WILL GIVE YOU MY WORD, YOU AND YOUR KIND WILL BE HELD IN MY HEART WITH HONOUR. I SHALL SET YOUR IMAGE ON MY LODGE WALL AS A MARK OF RESPECT.'

'*Then I will serve you well, my name is . . . Seal this in your heart and tell it to no one; now set me free.*'

Gently you untangle the creature from the thorn bush. In its struggle to be free it has been wounded and you take some of the blood on your finger and lick it, taking the essence of the animal into yourself. Then you offer your hand to the creature, which quickly and easily nips deep enough to draw a bead of blood and licks it up taking your essence into itself. You feel the creature's magical power flow into your heart, mind and soul. It is a power of life and of healing, of the knowledge of birth and how to die. Now you are of one blood, and one mind. You let your body flow into the shape-change, and now there are two creatures the same.

You pass into the forest and your totem brother/sister shows you its paths, water holes, and resting places. It teaches you the calls for danger, food, help, and mating, and the death song of its kind. Others come and you are made part of the company and share in the knowledge of the Group Mind. Finally, as the day draws to a close you are taken back to the point where this inner land joins the trunk of the Spirit Tree. You say farewell, rubbing your heads together, exchanging scent and touch. Then you take the path into the branches of the tree and as you do so, your shape flows back into that of a human being.

Slowly you climb down, and as you do, you begin to hear the drums, faintly at first and then louder and louder. They stop suddenly and you feel a swaying motion that gradually grows less and less and finally stops. Wait for a little while and then, without opening your eyes, listen for the small sounds of your own world. Identify them, and then start to move, first the feet, and then the legs, now the arms, but all very slowly. Now move your head back and forth on your neck and from side to side. Now draw in a deep breath and hold it for a few seconds, then force it hard, out of your lungs. Now open your eyes gradually, look straight in front of you, pause, then look left and right without turning your head. Now up, now down. Very gently lift your head, then your body, and finally sit up. Wait a while, then swing your legs to the ground and stand. Again wait a while, then walk a few steps, then across the room. Breathe deeply and slowly and make sure you are fully back in your own body.

When you feel able, have a small glass of milk and one dry biscuit, then try to sleep if you can. You will need to get back to a full eating régime as slowly as you came off it — do not make the mistake of going straight into a three big meals a day routine. On the Sunday take everything very easy, an egg for breakfast (boiled or scrambled, not fried). For lunch some clear soup, and one small piece of fish or chicken in the evening. Gradually replace the things you have taken out of your diet, adding some every two days, until you are back to normal.

Look for a figure or a detailed picture of your totem animal, and put it where you can see it every day. Find out all you can about it, its habits and ways. Honour your promise and each day as you rise and as you sleep send out a blessing to your totem. When you need to heal, recall the charge of power you exchanged and call it down into your head, your heart, and finally into your hands. Above all, remain true to your totem.

8. OTHER TRADITIONS

We tend to talk about the accepted 'Western Tradition' as if it alone stood for the whole of the Western Hemisphere. This is not strictly true. Within that term we can find many other traditions equally valid and equally workable by the trained ritualist. In fact, when we speak of the Western Tradition we are in fact generally referring to the relatively small portion of the whole that takes in the Celtic traditions, and the close traditions of European countries such as France, Brittany (for no true Breton counts himself French!), Spain, Italy, Germany, as well as of course the United States. Scandinavia has its own traditions, which range from the Norse to the Finno-Ugric. These in turn lead to the shamanistic. The Greek Tradition is in a class of its own, although like all the rest it does overlap others. Egyptian Tradition is unique too, but it includes the early Coptic which is highly interesting and on which very little research has been undertaken.

The traditions of Africa are almost unknown quantities to the average Western occultist, who generally knows only of its Voodoo aspects, which is a derivative of the original liberally mixed with orthodox Catholic symbology. Macumba is very similar, and evolved in much the same way.

Moving to the Near East, we come to the Islamic and Hindu Path with their attendant myths and symbols. Of the former, it is the Sufi Path that would be the nearest approximation to what we would term 'the occult'. In reality, however, to speak simply of East and West as though they are poles apart is quite wrong. All the traditions overlap at a great many points and hold within themselves a vast spectrum of ritual work — all of which can be explored with great effect no matter what tradition one is born into. Dion Fortune spoke of her willingness to 'take gold from Ophir and cedar from Lebanon' and I heartily concur with this attitude. I have found great pleasure and profit in studying and using the riches to be found in other Paths. The rituals that make up this part of the book, although they do not purport to be exact copies, are built according to the symbolic patterns of those traditions. I ask only that in using them you remember that they are as holy and as sacred as your own. Treat them with respect, approach them with reverence, and in due course their godforms will reveal themselves to you, and you will understand them. Then you will learn, as I did, of the Rainbow Thread underlying and connecting the many ways of man's worship of the One Primal Source.

Having said that, I must point out that although I have never accepted the idea that I must be confined into one tradition alone, I quickly found that there were natural limits beyond which, I was made to understand, it was unwise for me to travel. Having disregarded this advice a couple of times, I added greatly to my experience in the first two attributes of the true magician: discretion and discrimination. My late teacher W.E. Butler would have laughed heartily over those escapades. He always maintained that people learned much more from a bunch of burned fingers than they ever could from doing things right first time. 'When you do something well,' he once said to me, 'you add to your memory of the ritual. When you do it wrong, you learn to cope quickly and add to your understanding of the ritual.' He was a very wise man.

However, I did find that a lot of the other traditions could be used and have made a study of them. Very often in my workshops on ritual magic I will include either rituals, or lectures on them, or take my students on a pathworking built around the myth and symbology of the lesser-known and understood traditions. In this way they become familiar with ways other than those native to them. In the case of each of the following rites, I have used an essence rather than a genuine ritual, and there are several good reasons for this. Firstly, many of you using this book will be fairly new to the work, and this means it must be stepped down to the point where no whiplash effect will be too great. Secondly, there are full genuine rituals in the real tradition held in the hands of the priests and elders of the particular Path to which those rituals belong, and should you desire to learn them you must seek out for yourselves those who are able to teach you. That is the Law. In most cases, it will involve a period of study that will enable you to touch the core of that particular belief system, and in some cases entry into a school, order, or chapter, even if only on an honorary footing.

Should you decide at a later date to take such a step, remember that another tradition deserves the same attention, courtesy and dedication that you have given to your own Path. Sadly, there has been a decline in occult ethics as the study of the subject has become more widespread, and so I would stress that anything given to you under oath *must* be respected and not used or disclosed without express permission. Nor should you ever degrade the work for purposes of your own.

With some of the other traditions you can enhance the rituals by the use of masks, in fact almost any ritual, but particularly that type we term ritual drama, can be made highly effective by using masks. The interesting thing is that they wipe away the person beneath them and set the mind free to enter into the ritual deeper than ever before. You will find them especially useful for the Rainbow Serpent Celebration, and details about how to make them can be found in the last chapter, 'Ritual as an Art'.

I have been asked if it is wise to trust the godforms of other traditions, and whether it would not be safer to continue to use the Archangelic Guardians of the Christian faith even when pursuing a different tradition altogether. I can only say that if you are so distrustful of foreign godforms, or so unsure of yourself, then you had better pursue a less demanding study. Serious study of the tradition you propose to use should tell you whether it is a Way of Light or not. If it is, then by whatever name the god-source is known will be protection enough. A god or goddess is an emanation of That which willed the Universe into being. You are also part of That, and there is a point at which All is One. That being so, all you have to fear, at any time, is yourself, your lack of judgement and experience, your lack of self-knowledge. These are things that no one can teach you; they can only be found in your personal grail, on your own personal quest. Hopefully this book will act as the first signpost on that path.

THE NAVAHO TRADITION

A Healing Rite

Up to a short time ago — comparatively speaking — it was a common error to dismiss the spiritual life, beliefs, and practices of the American Indian as being almost non-existent. Thanks to the efforts and determination of a few people, it has now become clear that they had, and still have, a highly principled and far reaching tradition that deserves much wider recognition. Authors and researchers like Kluckhorn, Leighton, Paul, Radin, Ella Clark and G. Reichard, to name but a few, have sought out and recorded much that would otherwise have been lost for ever, but time is running out for the original races of North America, and some of the innermost teachings will die with the last shaman.

An undertaking as great as the creation of a new race, compressed into a few hundreds of years instead of the more usual thousands, must come through sacrifice. In much the same way that the Jews were, and sadly still are, the scapegoats of the Old World, so the Red Man was and is the scapegoat of the New. We cannot know what the inner levels had in mind when they started the trek to the New World from all over the Old, for this has not yet been revealed; but there is no doubt that there was, and still is, a purpose behind it. From a mere trickle of new arrivals during the first two hundred years or so, the number of immigrants swelled to a torrent of humanity from every country in the world, and North America, became a cauldron into which was being poured the ingredients for a new race. There are many who would scoff at this conception, and who sneer at the impetuosity and brashness of the young race; but just as every child goes through stages of growth, so does every race. Both grow eventually into adults and take their place among their peers.

However, the sacrifice must first be made. In the stories of the Grail we read of the mother giving the child to be offered up, and of that same child reappearing from the Chalice. To my way of thinking, this is the destiny of the American Indian. On the outer level he seems doomed, for whichever way he turns there he finds a new blind alley. If he integrates with other races he loses his pure blood; if he keeps himself to himself, the young people of his tribes will resent not having what they see, quite rightly, as being their share of freedom.

The Red Man may pass, but he will pass *into* the new race as its spiritual DNA. The wisdom and dignity of the Indian will form the basis on which a new stage in the development of the young race can be built. Thus by his sacrifice, the American Indian will be the saviour of the race.

The Mysteries of the American Indian have much to offer, even if one has no racial connection with them. Many tribes and nations inhabit the vast continent of America, but all share the belief that everyday life and religion are inextricably entwined, and that you cannot separate one from the other. It is a point of view that says: everything is holy in its way, and that what is seemingly opposite is there for a purpose, usually to bring its other side into sharper focus.

As far as we can tell — and there is a lot more still to be discovered — the Navaho nation originally came from a point in what is now central Siberia, over the land bridge that once covered the Bering Straits, and into the continent of America at its northernmost point. Even now the facial characteristics of the Athabascan people, of whom the Navaho form part, show this closeness of blood line and descent. The ancestors of the Navaho first settled in the north-west of Canada, and during the course of some several hundreds of years slowly drifted south, passing through the modern States of Washington and Oregon, down through California, crossing the Rockies and settling finally in the desert lands of Arizona and Utah. These tribes eventually became the Navaho and the Apache. Both tribes intermingled quite freely with the other tribes of the region; nevertheless, they kept their tribal identity with fierce determination. More than any other nation, they have resisted attempts to turn them into replicas of white men, and yet they are also fiercely loyal to their country. Many of them died in Vietnam proving it.

The Hollywood idea of the Red Indian, sullen and warlike, is in many cases a misinformation; certainly all the tribes were warlike, but only in defence of their lives, their families, and their right to live. Their famed cruelty — particularly in the case of the Apache — was learned at the hands of the invading Spaniards, who were at that time past masters in the art of torture. Mostly the Indian has a great sense of humour that belies his calm face and dignified manner, and this makes it all the more regrettable that so many of their young people — and some of the older ones as well — have fallen victim to alcoholism in modern times. For those who would like to know more of the true history of these amazingly talented people, R. Locke's *The Book of the Navaho*, published by Mankind Publishing Company, Los Angeles, California, is one of the best books on the subject ever written.

The Navaho call themselves 'The Dineh', which means 'the people', and their lands the 'Dinetah' or 'place of the people'. They have no word in their language for religion, but only a 'Way' of life, of living, loving, dying and being born, that is all contained in the *Rainbow Way*. The proud Dineh do not practise their religion, they *live* it. It would be impossible to put into one short chapter all that this Indian nation believe in; but their beautiful imagery and the effectiveness of their rites speak for themselves. Of all their symbols the most revered and the most used is that of the rainbow. To them it is *the* way of life. 'May you walk a rainbow path' is an often-used form of farewell. Their sayings are full of wisdom learned the hard way. 'Walk a mile in another man's shoes before you speak against him,' is one of them, and it makes a good seed thought for meditation. Almost everything has a song attached to it too, for music plays a great part in their lives. The Navaho are matrilineal in descent, and so the Mother is a very powerful symbol; both Earth Mother and Sun Father are strong images, as is the Corn Woman, or Changing Woman. Even now many of the older people still rise before dawn to say good morning to the sun (their father) and the earth (their mother).

One of the most important parts of the Navaho tradition is the use
of beautiful and intricate sand paintings, properly called dry paintings.
In these designs the people use symbols passed down to them for
thousands of years. Sand paintings are formed from many-coloured
sands, earths and seeds. Some of the symbols used follow the pattern
of symbols found all over the world, the Swastika and the Tree of Life
among many others.

Traditionally, pictures are started at dawn, used, and then destroyed
before sunset. Those seen in museums have been left partially unfinished
to comply with this belief. The paintings are used in many ways and
for all kinds of purposes, but primarily for healing. They are at once
Temples, in the sense that they represent a sacred enclosure, and an
altar on which offerings are made and to which men and women come
as suppliants. They are also used by the shaman or his patient as a
sacred seat, through which the vibrations of the symbols can be absorbed
into mind and body, thus eliminating disease or bad feeling and replacing
them with health and good feelings. It is this latter idea that you will
be using as a basis for your first step into 'other traditions'.

Coloured sands are rarely easily come by, but, as in all magical work,
intention is everything, and you can use coloured chalk or crayons.
Many other designs and symbols besides the one you are going to use
for the purposes of this chapter can be found in your local library, and
you can soon amass a good collection of suitable Navaho symbols for
future work. There is also a list of useful books at the end of the book
which should assist you considerably should you want to take up this
work in a serious way. Be sure, however, to get the colours you use
as close as you possibly can to the original design. The Dineh place
great value on colour, one of the most sacred being a clear turquoise.

On page 98 you will find a drawing of a sand painting which is used
to bring together the many parts of the soul. To reproduce it you will
need a large sheet of paper on which to make the drawing, and some
coloured chalk. For the actual ritual, it is best to wear an old pair of
jeans — you will be sitting down, and chalk rubs off. The background
colour in this instance is a pale gold, and the fourfold circle in the centre
is divided as follows: top segment, pale gold, then going around the
circle clockwise; second segment, black; bottom segment, grey and
remaining segment, white. These triangles are outlined in each other's
colour, so that the black segment will be outlined in white, the gold
outlined in grey, and so on. Each snake is coloured according to the
triangle from which it emerges, and again it should be outlined in one
of the other colours. The encircling snake should be black, outlined
in white. This is the Navaho version of the labyrinth, here seen as a

way back to self-integration, and it is held by them to be a particularly powerful symbol.

Try to keep to the tradition of painting the picture or symbol and then destroying it within twelve hours of the daylight time it was started. This is essential to the success of the ritual, as most of the intention of the actual rite is accomplished during its drawing out. It must be started and completed in one operation, so do not plan to go out to lunch in the middle. You must abstain from food while the painting is being drawn, though liquids may be taken. I suggest that it is permissible to trace out the drawing lightly the night before to make the process a little easier, but if it can be done completely in one day this is by far the best course and does make a difference. While working, try to hold in the mind the thought that this is a picture of the symbolic journey of your soul back to its source, where it may draw strength, life force, and the ability to cope with life in general. Before you begin painting, make sure that what will become the white triangle is facing east.

Once you have completed the painting, and feel you have embodied the main intention of the ritual in its symbolism, then you can complete the ceremony, first preparing the place of working as usual. Because you will be working in the Navaho tradition, you should use their godforms and symbols for the four quarters.

The main symbol of the ritual is a spiral, which is an ancient and very important symbol all over the world, so the opening sigil will be that of a spiral made by pointing the finger and, starting from the centre in a clockwise direction, working outward to a distance of about eighteen inches, then moving the fingers back to the centre, when you should pronounce the god name of that particular quarter before moving on, hand and finger still extended, to the next quarter.

As always, start in the east, using the name of 'White Shell Woman'. 'Turquoise Woman' is the name for the south, 'Salt Woman' the name for the west, and 'Spider Woman' the name for the north. These are all aspects of Changing Woman, one of the main godforms of the Navaho. It is through the transforming influence of the feminine aspect that the ritual works. (A more complicated form of preparing the quarters is to 'raise the sky' on four wands of shell, turquoise, black and gold, but this requires more information than space permits here.)

Once the place is prepared, sit in the middle of the picture. Let the energy you have painted into it enter your body through the chakra at the base of the spine. Bear in mind that you are aiming for the integration of self and wholeness of spirit. Keep as tight a mental hold on these concepts as you can. Let the benign power of the symbols

The Healing Shield

mount slowly along your spine like a gentle warmth. It should feel rather like a rising tide of warm water. *Do not imagine it as a fire*. Let it emerge from the head centre in the form of three eagle feathers. Concentrate on holding this image for as long as you can. Then, by will and intent, seal off the point of entry from the painting.

After a short period, rise and close the quarters, making the spiral sigils again, this time from the *outside* point to the centre, thanking each godform as you go, and giving each permission to depart. Having made certain that the centres are securely closed, you can make your usual report.

I must emphasize that this is but a pale representation of the original, very powerful, Navaho rite, which has a special chant to go with it. However, to use this chant properly, one would have to learn it direct from a shaman, and one, moreover, who was prepared to teach it correctly. At least in this form, the ritual will link you with another tradition, and you will grow by the experience.

THE SLAVONIC TRADITION

Earth Mother Rite

The magical traditions of Western Europe are peopled with strange and endearing creatures. Who could fail to be intrigued by Domovois and Bannicks, Ovinniks and Kikimoras? Mind you, some of these little creatures need to be handled with care, but on the whole they play the same role in rustic life as do the brownies and house fairies of Britain.

There is very little left of the Slavonic tradition. For the most part its originators were farmers and lived in harsh conditions with little to be joyful about and much to fear, and thus many of the little rustic divinities of this tradition were seen as being helpful to a household only if they were treated with respect. If this proved in any eventuality not to be the case, dire consequences resulted. In the main, however, the actual mythology of the Slavs is as nebulous as the mists that cover their marsh-ridden lands. To begin with, the Slavic people inhabit several countries and speak several different languages. The people of Poland, the Ukraine, Latvia and Lithuania all form part of the Slav nation, and were all at one time under different governments than the ones presently obtaining. Their belief system is more closely akin to shamanism than anything else, but it contains portions of other traditions picked up from peoples that have passed through their lands at one time or another.

The foundation of the Slavonic Way seems to be an early form of dualism, which bears close resemblance to the Persian version and the gods Ormuzd and Ahriman. In the Slavonic tradition, these two gods are referred to simply as Byelobog (White God) and Charnobog (Black God). All natural events were seen as being due to the conflict between these two gods. There was also a sky god, Svarog, whose name has a Sanskrit root *svar*, meaning bright or clear, and from Svarog came Dazhbog, the Sun, and Svarogich, fire. The Slavs held fire in healthy respect. The root of the name Svarogich is Ogon, the whole name meaning bright fire. It is very near to the Sanskrit *Agni*. The lighting of the first fire in a new home was a special event, as we shall see later.

Strangely, in most parts of the area designated as being Slavonic, the Moon was a male divinity. In at least one myth he is described as the Sun's 'old bald Uncle'. The Sun reigned over 12 kingdoms (the zodiac) and was attended by two maidens, the Aurora of the Morning, and the Aurora of the Evening. To confuse things still further, in other regions the Sun was a young child who was born in the morning, grew through the day, and died at sunset. Yet other regions speak of the Sun as a handsome young man with the Moon as his consort. The whole thing is very mixed up.

However, let us turn to the subject of this chapter, the little rustic divinities who played such a large part in the daily life of the community. Most of these creatures were seen as being the children of Mati-Syra-Zemyla, 'Mother Earth Moist'. When Christianity was brought to the Slavs, the great gods died, but the little ones survived, and even to this day living remnants can be found in more remote areas. Chief among them was the Domovoi, a house brownie as we would call him. *Dom* means house, and the Domovoi lived under the stove. He was sometimes called 'Grandfather', or 'the Little Master', or — and very strangely since the only other race to use the same appellation is the Irish — 'Himself '.

If you were lucky enough to see 'Himself ', you would see a vaguely human little being, covered with fine silky hair, although sometimes he could appear as an animal or a bundle of hay in a corner. He had a soft voice, and in the night could be heard groaning and calling to himself in the kitchen. His favourite places were under the stove or under the threshold stone. When a young couple were married and built a new home, the young bride would lay a fire in her new stove, and then take a firebrand from her old home and run with it to light the new fire. As soon as the stove was hot enough, she would bake a batch of bread

'Himself'

and the first slice would be placed under the stove and the door left open all night. This was to attract a Domovoi who as yet had no home. Sometimes the bride would simply bring with her a slice of bread from her old home and place it beneath the stove or hearthstone in her new one. In return for warmth, and the first slice of any bread baked in the house, the Domovoi would look after the house. He acted rather like a Celtic Bean-sidhe, and would weep and wail if a death or illness was in the offing. He would also gently pull the wife's hair to warn her if her husband was in a bad mood or likely to beat her. The Domovoi had a female equivalent, the Domovikha, but she preferred to live in the cellar and watch over the stores there.

The yard spirits were a little less friendly. They never came into the house, and kept themselves to themselves. There was the Dvorovoi (from *dvor*, meaning yard), who would get very upset if the yard was not kept swept and tidy. As this was considered to be a child's work, it was a convenient way of getting the children to do their chores. If they knew that the Dvorovoi would keep them awake all night weeping under their window, they were much less likely to leave something not done!

The Dvorovoi yard spirit hated any animal with white fur — we are not told why — and to appease him a little sheep's wool and a few glittering beads with a slice of bread had to be placed in the yard or over the door of the stable. When making this offering, one had to sweet-talk the little spirit, calling him 'neighbour' and asking his help in the care of the yard animals. If, however, the Dvorovoi got out of hand one could give him a bad fright by hanging up the body of a dead magpie in the yard instead.

Then there was the Bannik (*banya* means bath). He lived in the bathhouse, which was usually located a little way from the house, rather like a modern sauna. There was a strict order of etiquette here; the Bannik would allow three groups of people to bathe, but then the bathhouse had to be left to him and his friends. The forest spirits and such could then come and have their bath and use the bathhouse like a social club to exchange gossip and talk of their own ways. A little water was always left for the Bannik's use, otherwise he got very upset and made life difficult by hiding clothes and towels. He could, if he was in a good mood, be asked about the future, although my guess is that few people would care to apply the necessary method of asking, since this entailed putting one's bare behind through the open door of the banya. If you got your behind scratched it was a bad omen. If the Bannik stroked you gently, things were going to go well.

The Ovinnik (*ovin* means barn) usually took the form of a large black cat and lived in the barn. However, the Ovinnik could also bark like a dog or laugh like a man. A somewhat confusing mixture, he was badly behaved most of the time, and was usually blamed for any fires started in the barn. Of all the little house gods he was the most irritating.

One spirit only was female, apart from the wife of the Domovoi, and that was the Kikimora. Sometimes her duties included looking after the poultry, but she would also help in the house if the wife was a hard-working girl and diligent. If she was not, however, the Kikimora made her life even harder by strewing the house with mud and dust. The Kikimora also liked to tickle the children in their sleep and make them laugh.

It is now time to think about a simple ritual that we can adapt for your use from the Slavonic tradition. There are two that are suitable, the first being a simple protection ritual that could well be used by anyone living in a farming area or near open spaces of woodland, and the other is to be used for the calling of a Domovoi to live in the house, which in this sense can be seen in the same light as a house brownie.

For the first, protective, ritual you should wait for the first day of the harvest month of August, when you should rise before dawn and go into the fields with someone of the opposite sex carrying a jar of oil. When you have chosen your spot, and just before the sun comes up, *you* should make the following invocation to the Earth Mother:

'MATI-SYRA-ZEMYLA, MOTHER OF US ALL, BEFORE THY SON THE SUN LEAVES HIS PALACE, HEAR US WHO CALL TO THEE. WE WOULD THANK THEE FOR ALL THAT HAS BEEN GIVEN TO US AND WOULD IMPLORE THY PROTECTION FROM THE DARKNESS OF WINTER.'

The man should then lie down upon the earth after you have carved with a new knife an equal-armed cross under the spot in which he will lie. He should lie with his head to the east, and feet to the west. The woman should then take the jar of oil and pour some of it out at his head, saying:

'MATI-SYRA-ZEMYLA, MOIST MOTHER EARTH, TURN EVERY EVIL THING THAT MAY COME UPON US, MAKE US STRONG SO THAT IT MAY NOT BE ABLE TO HARM OUR FAMILY OR ANIMALS.'

She should then walk to the south and again pour oil onto the earth, saying:

'MATI-SYRA-ZEMYLA, MOIST MOTHER EARTH, TURN AWAY ALL UNCLEAN THINGS THAT WE MAY REMAIN PURE IN THY SIGHT. LET US BE MADE CLEAN BEFORE YOU.'

The oil should then be taken to the west and once more a libation should be made, saying:

'MATI-SYRA-ZEMLYA, MOIST MOTHER EARTH, TURN AWAY FROM US BAD WEATHER AND STRONG WINDS. ALL THE FORCES OF THE SKY AND THE LIGHTNING TURN AWAY FROM US THAT WE MAY BE HELD SAFE IN THY HANDS.'

Lastly, the woman should go to the north, and after the oil has been poured, say:

'MATI-SYRA-ZEMYLA, MOIST MOTHER EARTH, MAKE THE NORTH WIND GENTLE. TURN THE SNOW KING FROM HIS PATH ACROSS OUR LAND. KEEP SAFE THE LAMB AND THE COW AND THE GOAT. SHOW US MERCY MOIST MOTHER EARTH.'

Finally, the jar should be broken and buried in the earth, and you should both return home without looking back.

Sometimes this ritual was done by four people, each person taking one direction, and kneeling down with their faces pressed to the earth as the oil was poured and the invocation made. There are older versions of this ritual too, which seem to pre-date the Corn King/Spring Queen ceremonies in which the act of fertility is the culmination of the ritual. In this it is similar in some ways to some of the rites of the Craft.

The second ritual is that in which the Domovoi or house spirit is drawn into the home to act as a guardian. Here, however, I would add a word of warning. Once you have invited such an entity into your house, remember that it will not tolerate untidiness, neglect or disinterest in its presence. If you want to enjoy the company of a house brownie, all well and good. Just remember that henceforth you will be responsible for keeping him sweet-tempered and active. You are also responsible for giving him a good example, for all elementals learn from those human beings to whom they become attached. To teach an elemental bad ways carries a heavy Karma. However, if you decide that you do have room for one small hairy being to live under your stove, here is a modern variation of the old ritual.

The most important requirement is a sympathetic friend or relative whose home you regard as being warm, friendly, and all you would wish a home to be. With their permission and blessing, bake a batch of bread in their oven. Before you turn off the heat, have ready a covered lamp with which you may carry a light taken from the oven of your friend to your own house. Before you leave with a crust of the bread and the light, you should make a small invocation. First, open all the doors throughout the house (it is best to wait until summer to do this) and have someone at your own home with the doors open, and then say:

'MALE DZIADEK [*marleh jadek* means little grandfather], OUR HOUSE IS LONELY, THE SPACE BENEATH THE STOVE IS COLD. COME WITH THE BREAD AND THE LIGHT TO OUR HOUSE AND LIVE IN PEACE WITH US. SEE, THE DOOR LIES OPEN, LITTLE MASTER OF THE STOVE. COME AND LIVE WITH US, GUARD US IN THE DARKNESS OF THE NIGHT AND BE PART OF OUR FAMILY. FOLLOW THE BREAD AND THE LIGHT AND DO NOT BE AFRAID LITTLE GRANDFATHER.'

Then you should take the light and bread to your own home, entering through the open doors and leaving them open. Go to the kitchen (which must be neat and clean) and place the bread under the stove or oven, or at the back if it is not possible to get underneath. Light the oven with the light from the other house, and say:

'MALE DZIADEK, WELCOME TO YOUR NEW HOME, WELCOME TO YOUR NEW COMPANIONS. BREAD IS WAITING FOR YOU AND A WARM STOVE TO LEAN AGAINST. SEE, THE DOORS ARE OPEN. BRING GOOD LUCK, LONG LIFE AND HAPPINESS INTO THIS HOUSE WITH YOU, BE OUR GUARDIAN AND OUR FRIEND. WELCOME, LITTLE GRANDFATHER, WELCOME.'

On the first day of each month thereafter you should replace the bread with a new crust, and on high days and holidays leave a small glass of wine on the floor near the stove for the Domovoi. *Always* tell him anything of importance that is going to happen in the family, and *always* remember he is there and address him, if only occasionally. If you leave the house, *remember to take your Domovoi with you*! Do not forget to take him, or both you and the new tenants will regret it.

One last piece of information concerning the Slavonic tradition. In the remote villages in times of plague, the old women would summon all the other women and from them would choose nine virgins and three widows. These women would then go to the edge of the village, and here they would strip and loose their hair. The virgins would then be harnessed to a plough, one of the widows would drive it, and the other two would urge on these human 'horses' with whips. The plough would be driven round the village three times to form a barrier across which the evil could not come. Older and darker versions of this rite required that one man be spreadeagled at each corner of the village, and the plough would be driven over him, literally ploughing him into the ground as a sacrifice. No one knew who these men were until everyone returned to their homes afterward. Only the old women knew which men had been chosen. This practice came to Britain in a very similar form along with the Celts after they had wandered through this part of Europe, and is found in the darker annals of Devonshire and Cornwall.

We condemn such things from our more enlightened era and our newer ways of living, but we must remember that these people were primitive and ignorant in many ways — although wise in many others. They did what they saw as being all they could do, and out of such things has grown a finer understanding of the pressures under which they lived. It is easy to condemn, standing as we do far away in time. It is hard for us to understand the horrors that were wrought so long ago. Yet even in modern man there is a savage lurking not too far beneath the surface, and in the darker pathologies of the mind there still lurk the fears and desperation of primitive man.

9. THE SONG OF THE RAINBOW SERPENT

THE STORYTELLER

The art of the storyteller is fast dying out. In Ireland the few Seanachaid left are the last of their kind, and the travelling tellers of tales are almost forgotten. But there are a few pockets of resistance still left. In Australia, Moses Aaron is a modern-day Bard, travelling to schools, community centres, church halls and fairs to tell his stories. Television and radio have also given him the opportunity to reach people all over that vast land, a land which is itself the home of many a fine storyteller, the Aboriginal Tribesman. Within the tradition of magic we have the pathworking, a story built within the kingdom of the mind and a part of magic itself, but there is a place for the traditional 'telling of tales and weaving of dreams'. The following is something I often use to end a workshop, for it sends people home in a relaxed and happy mood, feeling that they have contributed to the whole of the three or five days.

You certainly do not need the 'Rainbow Serpent' staff that I use — you can use any staff, a wand, or even an object that is significant to the group. There must, however, be something that can be handed on to another person. I use a wooden snake, hand-carved in Australia by a Tribesman and now attached to a staff. I have a collar of many coloured ribbons that is tied around the serpent head giving it a rainbow cloak of many colours. In Celtic lands the Master Bards also wore cloaks of many colours, a garment that distinguished them from other classes and made them easily seen in a crowded hall lit only by rush lamps.

You must first choose a theme and make sure either by talking or reading out some of the main myths that the group has enough knowledge of that theme to take on the serpent staff. It is at its most atmospheric if you are outside on a summer or autumn night, sitting round a fire. There must be enough room for each 'teller' to walk around the circle, and the rules are simple; no one is allowed to refuse to speak

'Once Upon a Time . . .'

and you must make a minimum and a maximum time allowable for people to speak. I find a minimum of five minutes and a maximum of ten sufficient for most groups. This means that a shy or inexperienced speaker is not made uncomfortable, and a more fluent one is given enough time to develop an idea. You, of course, can decide your own times for you will know your own group and its capabilities.

The leader of the group starts and ends the story. If you like you can have a small bell to hand and ring it at five and again at ten minutes to give the speaker an indication of how much time he or she has. The art is in giving a good enough start, one that offers several paths down which the narrative can meander. When experience is gained the whole thing can be turned into an evening of enchantment and competition with the best storytellers vying with one another to weave the best or the most complicated story and, inevitably, to leave the one coming after in the biggest difficulty. A small prize for the best, chosen by acclaim, can then round off the evening.

To give everyone a chance it is a good idea to choose the theme ahead of time and let everyone know. This means they can research it and dig up information for themselves as well as the basics given to them already. A central piece such as a fire is important but, if this is impossible, then I suggest a cauldron or a large punch bowl filled with red wine or real punch. As each speaker finishes his or her part of the tale they can collect a paper cup and dip it into the wine and refresh a dry throat. You will have to make up your own mind if applause will be allowed at the end of each speaker, or if it should be simply a continuous thing.

As the leader, you start by taking hold of the staff/object and beginning to pace around the circle. Later on, when the whole idea is familiar, you can enact your story, using mime and gestures to enhance your telling. You can go even further and supply some masks (see Chapter 10), leaving them in a heap in the centre and letting the storytellers choose a mask. This can help a shy speaker, and give a dramatic tool to the more experienced one. Walk slowly around the circle, every now and then shaking the serpent staff, making it seem as if it too was listening. Then start to lay your opening scene, as in a pathworking. Your audience needs to have descriptive data with which everyone can build the images in their minds. This is the art of a true storyteller — you listen with your mind's eye, not simply with your ears.

Bring in your first character. Be careful not to introduce too many or you will get confused and leave the next speaker with a well nigh impossible task to keep track of them. Try to build up the tension towards a peak; then stop and hand over the staff to someone else. They must now get up and take your place and carry on the story. The point of every story is that, in one way or another, it is the story of the hero/heroine who walks the path of life and learns through many experiences, before finally reaching the goal of the Quest. You can weave in as many of the classical confrontations as you wish, but you must remain within the original tradition — you cannot pass from Egyptian to Greek to Shamanic. However, you can use the ancient symbols of the Wise Woman, the forest, the totem animal, the sword/chalice, the battle, the encounter with the shadow, the castle, and so forth. The story must follow through, it must make sense, and later on, when it becomes a competition as well as for enjoyment, you must pull up a speaker if they wander off into nonsense and make them start afresh.

This kind of mini-ritual is something that can be used with children. It will keep them quiet for hours as well as teach them to concentrate, think ahead and plan in a logical manner, and will give them an incentive to look up and read about the characters they will be using. It can be adapted to any age from kindergarten to retirement homes. It can be used in therapy and in counselling. The story is the universal symbol and gradually the speaker will come to understand that the story they tell is drawing on their own deeply hidden desires, needs and fears, and that, in bringing them to the surface through the medium of the story, they are acting them out and setting them free.

When the last speaker finishes and you, as leader, take back the staff, it is your task to bring the whole thing to a full circle and sum it all up. This may only need a few minutes, or the last speaker could well have left you in a real pickle. But end it you must, and with no loose ends. A word of warning — this storytelling can become addictive!

10. RITUAL AS AN ART

Too often the practice of ritual is regarded as being akin to joining an amateur dramatic society. Nothing could be further from the truth. To give ritual the attention, power and dignity it deserves, one should serve an apprenticeship with a master magician. Unfortunately this ideal condition is very rarely possible, but you should at least approach the art with a sense of respect, making a sincere effort to learn all its facets, and attempting to see it for what it is — a means of concentrating the mind and achieving oneness with the higher self. You should always remember that the gods and goddesses with whom you are working are all to be found *within you* as the magician. You and you alone, if you are working solo, will be their point of manifestation, and all the forms, images and results will come to earth through you and those who may be working with you. Because of this, it is essential that you understand that what *you* are within will colour all those forms accordingly. Therefore, if something manifests that is not in accordance with the way you have planned things, then before you blame anything or anyone . . . look to yourself. Power can only manifest and focus through a channel, and if there is anything in that channel that can be picked up on the way, it will be. Any results occurring in your Temple, Lodge, or sacred enclosure will *always* have overtones of your personality. It therefore makes it imperative that any would-be magician makes his inner self as balanced and as harmonious as possible.

You may say that it is all very well for me to give you such advice from the relatively safe viewpoint of many years of experience, but if it is any consolation *all* magicians make mistakes, no matter how many years they have been working at their craft. All experience will do for you is to enable you to mitigate any harmful results. Do not give up if you find things difficult for the first six months or so. You will learn from mistakes just as much as you will learn from doing things just right. A successful ritual will improve your memory, increase your confidence, and probably get you a good result. An unsuccessful ritual will teach you caution, give you an understanding of the forces you have misplaced, test your courage and your ability to deal with the unexpected. It will also teach you how to cope with the panic that can ensue among those working with you at the time. Balanced against each other, these latter points are as instructive and useful as the former.

Also remember when working with others to choose only those people you trust, or you will find details of your activities all over the local press, and your so-called friend will be collecting on your embarrassment. Do *not* let all and sundry know what you are doing, or where your interests lie. Thoroughly test any new friendship that might lead you to offer an invitation to join in your Lodge. Remember that in all your magical work you are only as strong as your weakest link. You cannot always blame the group member who cracks. It may be that you overtaxed his or her strength without first trying to find their breaking point. It is difficult sometimes, especially when you are some way into your work and things are going well, to keep your elation and happiness to yourself. There is an urge to share this new-found joy (and certainly the work brings much joy) with everyone around you. This is a natural feeling. It is also your first test. Discretion and discrimination are the virtues most needed here. Discipline this urge and train yourself to listen, observe and wait until the right people come along. You can actually do people a disservice by 'awakening' them too soon.

Not all ritual is as gentle or as innocuous as those I have given in this book — far from it. In fact, with this new edition you will find some of the new rituals pack quite a hefty punch. There are rituals, and you may come across some of them in the future, that would test the courage of the stoutest heart, not because of any horror brought into form but because of an old-fashioned thing called *awe*. This is seldom understood, but there is no way to describe to another human being what happens when this emotion manifests in a Temple. It is hard to breathe, there is a pressure that builds and builds in your physical and mental bodies. There is fear, but of a different kind to any other. There is also an exaltation that brings one at times dangerously close to a death-wish simply because the level reached — for a few brief moments in time — is so high that leaving it is an intolerable thought. These are the moments when something, some entity, enters the sphere of the Temple, and is of such a high intensity that the human nervous system can barely exist alongside it. Fortunately, most of the time these beings are well aware of the effect they have upon us and will lower that intensity to allow a brief period of mutual awareness. It is during those times that new ideas, thoughts, plans and methods of future teaching are passed from one plane to another.

There are, on the other hand, odd moments when, because of sloppy preparation, entities arrive that are not what was originally invited. This type of being, particularly if it is elemental in nature, is not always aware of the inability of human beings to cope with other levels of existence. That is when you find yourself in trouble, and it is one of the reasons for never dealing directly with an elemental. You should always work through the appropriate Elemental King, or through one of the Archangelic Regents. On the other hand, you should not make the mistake of thinking that elementals are necessarily evil. Out of their natural element they are as unhappy to be with you as you are to see them! If such an entity should appear uninvited, your first need will be to contact the King or Regent of that particular element and request that they come and collect that which belongs to them. At the same time, you should offer an apology for causing such a misplacement of force. Courtesy has its place on the inner levels every bit as much as on the physical plane, and, along with ethics and correct behaviour, is as vital a part of the art of ritual.

Train yourself to patience; learn slowly and with thoroughness and don't be afraid of mistakes. There is no way anyone can teach another how to cope in ritual emergencies. It is very much a do-it-yourself situation. All anyone can tell you is do not panic and start your career as a magician slowly and build up to greater things. Learn from anything that goes wrong. Try to find out where the departure from the norm occurred. Keep a meticulous diary, covering all your rituals, even the smallest. Make everyone working with you hand in a report as soon as possible — not more than 36 hours after the ritual took place. Do not file these reports away unread; study them and compare them over a period of time, each against the other. See who works best at what point, and try to encourage them to improve in those areas where they are least effective. Encourage those who seem to be holding back, and gently discipline those whose enthusiasm seems ready to burst its bounds. Do not put up with sloppy work, sporadic attendance, inattention or rudeness. Ritual is not a game — such things can cause dangerously weak points in your circle.

You as Magus or High Priestess are not exempt. Your report is the most important. Never be too proud to accept advice or a good idea from a younger or less experienced member — sometimes an inner level prompting will be sent through such a person. You may also find you have a 'silent power point' in your group. These are people who do not appear, on the surface, to be doing very much, and they are seldom very good as officers, yet when they do not attend for whatever reason the rituals seem flat. Such people are valuable, for they act as storage batteries for power. It is their placid and even nature that enables them to take quite large amounts of power, usually without knowing it, and feed it through into the rituals. For important seasonal rituals, place them in the north and watch the power go round like a piston engine. After a year of working you will be able to pinpoint those in the group who have potential and those who are content simply to serve without ambition. Both are important.

Enjoy your rituals; they should be a source of great happiness and strength and add to your fullness of life. There are some rituals that are usually seen as being more subdued, such as the preparing of the way for one who has passed the portals of life into the West, or sometimes — in the case of an initiate — someone who is preparing to leave on that journey. Such rituals are openings through which the prepared soul may slip gently and easily away. However these can be highly specialized rituals, and not to be undertaken unless one has been taught personally by someone who is a trained Priest of Anubis, or, in a different tradition, Persephone. There are also rituals that will free those who are enclosed in their own darkness, and such rituals can incur danger to those who work them, and there are cleansing rituals for places that have been misused by dark forces. All these must be learned at the shoulder of a master craftsman or woman; they are *not* for beginners and cannot be learned (except as theory) from a book.

Come to all your rituals with an open mind. Do not turn away from the gods of others, for a competent magician should be able to work across the board, using Greek, Egyptian, Celtic, Craft, Hindu, Qabalistic or American Indian traditions, to name but a few. The only criteria is that the tradition learned is used as a Way of Light. Such ability will not happen in a few weeks or months or even years, so count on continuing to learn for the rest of your life. Grades, levels and strange insignia have little or no value unless they are ratified by inner-level experience. You will always know a true magician. He or she will not be concerned with such titles. That is not what the work is about. True position is shown by lifestyle and ability. If you enter a group or a school look first at the type of people it is turning out. Do they work well together? Are they happy in themselves? Does the school take note of your questions? Do you have a personal tutor with whom you can exchange views? All these things are pointers to training that will bring results. Note also how your teachers present themselves. Remember that the outward appearance of a person can be a pointer to the state of their inner self. All things in magic move from the inner state to the outer. If your bedroom looks like a bomb site, then it is time you looked at the state of your inner kingdom! True position is shown by a dignified lifestyle, ability and character.

Preparation is your best friend. Make certain you know all about the tradition of the godform you are using for a particular ritual. Build up a reference library. It does not have to contain thousands of books or even rare and out-of-print editions. You need comprehensive world mythologies, and one or two informative titles on the various disciplines within magic — Tarot, Gemstones, Talismans, Astrology, Geomancy, Numerology, Healing, etc. A basic work and one that is more advanced and offers a good bibliography is all you require. Include good occult fiction, which is often a good way to learn, for if the writer is also a practitioner, he or she will be writing from inner knowledge.

Buy the best you can afford, but do not pay for things you can make yourself. Buy only when you do not have either the knowledge or the skill that is needed. Books can be obtained from, among others, Mysteries, 9 Monmouth St, London, and from Watkins in Cecil Court, also in London. Arcania of 17 Union Passage, Bath, offers a wide range of books, implements, incenses and all you will need in magical work. as well as courses in a wide variety of occult skills. Star Child in Glastonbury specializes in oils and incense, and the doyen of incense makers is Margaret Bruce of High Rigg Farm, St John's Chapel, Bishop Auckland, in Durham. If you cannot thread a needle and do not know one end of a paper pattern from the other, write to Mysteries of Avalon, 32 Hamdon Close, Stoke-sub-Hamdon, Somerset who can make your robe. Occultique, 73 Kettering Road, Northampton, carries a wide range of occult supplies. Many publishers of New Age books offer a comprehensive catalogue of their current titles. You can find all these and more in the UK Directory of the Esoteric and Complementary Medicines, published by Lattimer Publications, Lattimer House, 14 Hilary Park, Douglas, Isle of Man, and I suspect there are similar publications for other countries of the world.

When working, check and recheck your symbology, colours, and your equipment. Make your fellow workers do the same. Consider each ritual as being of vital importance and make it as beautiful and dignified as possible. Take the trouble to learn your lines if it is possible, and move with grace and intent for you are among the immortals. Move the work around — do not appoint yourself Magus for life! Train everyone to take every part in Temple work. Learn all there is to learn about each point of contact. Being an Officer of the South is very different to controlling the Gate of the West. Research into new ways of ritual; consider for instance the psychological impact of ritual drama and

1

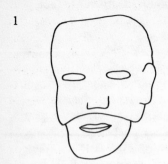

2

CUT AWAY BOTTOM
OF MASK

ATTACH BROAD ELASTIC
BEHIND TO GIVE FIRM HOLD

3

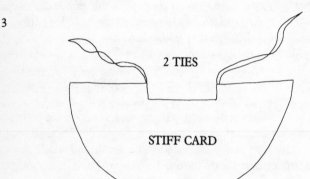

2 TIES

STIFF CARD

CUT OUT A SEMICIRCLE OF STIFF CARD AND ATTACH TWO TIES

4   5

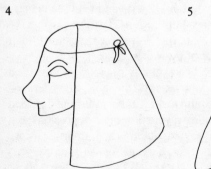

PLACE AGAINST FOREHEAD
AND TIE BEHIND HEAD
UNDER NEMYSS

DECORATE YOUR MASK
AS REQUIRED

working with masks. Egyptian rituals can be enormously enhanced with the use of such things. As mentioned in Chapter 3, Theatre Zoo of Earlham Street, London, has a wide variety of animal and human masks and with only a little time and effort you can make up a complete set. Cut away the bottom half of the mask for easier voice projection — this applies equally to human masks. Spray either gold or silver and outline the eyes in black, Egyptian fashion. Add a silk or cotton nemyss head-dress and you have something that will lift your ritual into something you never expected. For the gods who do not wear animal heads you will heighten the effect by painting face-masks with designs and adding sequins, beads, etc. The head-dresses are simple to add. I place a cheap brooch or coloured feathers on the brow of the nemyss or add tassels at the side. With these you need only a plain black robe, the plainness adding to the effect of the mask. A jackal head can be made by using a fox mask painted black and the eyes outlined in gold, as described in Chapter 3. Do not forget to paint the inside of the ears and nostrils also in gold. A lion mask for Amun Ra, a cow's for Hathor, a cat for Bast. For the Hawk Head of Ra you can use a parrot mask and cut away the bottom part of the beak, and spray it gold. I use these in workshops all over the world and it is always a success with those participating. I even take them over to America, and they will take a little battering. Plain face masks, suitably painted and with beards and perhaps crêpe hair wig pieces make effective Greek masks, and of course for shamanic work they are almost a must. The cost is not out of reach unless, as I need to do, you buy them for workshops of 40 or more people. You will need to practise using them. The head must be tilted back slightly when speaking to allow the voice to carry, and be sure to strengthen any elastic straps to make them firm. The only drawback of using masks is the heat. You will sweat gallons, but the overall effect is worth it. If you do not want to go to the trouble of the masks, try simple face make-up in varying colours — green and blue for the gods with body-paint designs added. You are limited only by your imagination; use it, it will take you to the gods.

Where robes are concerned there is a good basic pattern put out by Macalls Pattern Books, number 2066. This gives a basic robe pattern and a number of variations of wraps, hoods, cloaks, etc. For those of you who need to know addresses of craftspeople willing to make every kind of implement, robe, incense, or ritual object, write with an SAE to Spiral Publications at 8 King St, Glastonbury, BA6 9YJ, and ask how to obtain a copy of their Directory of Occult resources. UK price at the time of writing is £1.50.

Whatever you do or however you conduct your rituals, never let up

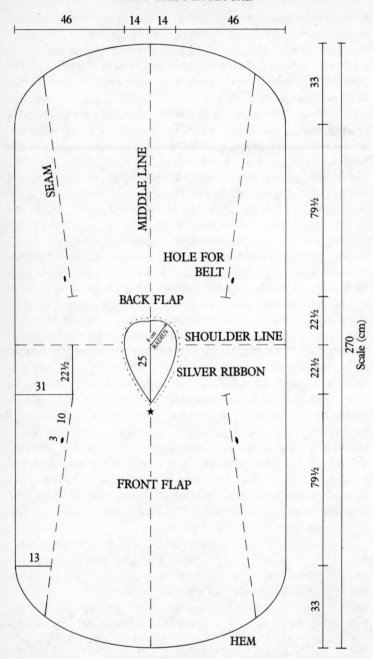

Robe of heavy black silken lining

on looking for more harmony within yourself. It is a foundation for the successful Lodge. Keep to your daily disciplines, and seek newer and deeper levels within yourself, and apply them to your Temple work. Remember, strictly speaking, no one can ever be a Master of ritual, for as you achieve the highest levels of one grade, you begin at the foot of the next one.

The best laid rituals can have their minor disasters and their hilarious moments. If in difficulty or doubt, invoke the Angel of the Temple and ask for help. Do not make your request a long-winded prayer: you can cut it down to a single word like 'Help!' if you like. If, as can happen, something funny occurs, treat it as a happy moment, and share it with the unseen companions you have invited to join you. Inner plane people have just as much sense of humour as we do — possibly more! Mix dedication with love and laughter. In ancient times the great annual rituals were times of great joy, and we have grown over-solemn in the years of the Piscean Age. The art of ritual is very much linked to the art of living.

You may go on and become a Master Magician; you may decide to become an armchair occultist and look on from afar; you may even give it up entirely — but you will never regret the time spent in ritual work, for through it you will come to know and understand yourself. The whole of life around you is part of a much greater ritual called evolution, one that started many millions of years ago. The officers and traditions change with the Dance of the Ages, but its intention is simple — the eventual bringing together of the Divine Whole. It is enough simply to have been a small part of that intention.

SERVANTS OF THE LIGHT is a school of occult science founded by the late W.E. Butler. For details of its correspondence course of instruction, apply to the Director of Studies, S.O.L., P.O. Box 215, St Helier, Jersey, Channel Islands, UK. Please include S.A.E. in UK, $2 currency USA.

The Ride of the Wild Hunt

BIBLIOGRAPHY

Qabalistic
The Magician: His Training and Work, W.E. Butler, Aquarian Press, 1959.
Apprenticed to Magic, W.E. Butler, Aquarian Press, 1981.
Practical Guide to Qabalistic Symbolism, G. Knight, Weiser, 1965.
Building a Temple, D. Ashcroft-Nowicki, SOL Publications, 1974.
The Secret Temple, R. Wang, Weiser.
The Magical Philosophy, Dennings and Phillips, Llewelyn, 1974.
Experimental Magic, J.H. Brennan, Aquarian Press, 1978.
Astral Doorways, J.H. Brennan, Aquarian Press, 1980.
The Inner Guide Meditation, E. Steinbrecher, Aquarian Press, 1982.
The Art of True Healing, I. Regardie, Weiser, 1969.
Secret Wisdom, D. Conway, Aquarian Press, 1987.
Any of the books of Shimon Ben Halevi.

Egyptian
Egyptian Magic, W. Budge, Dover, 1971.
Egyptian Magic, F. Farr, Aquarian Press, 1982.
Egyptian Book of the Dead, W. Budge, Dover, 1967.
Goten und Symbole der Alten Agypter, M. Hurkel, Barth Verlag, 1974.
Secrets of Egypt for the Millions, M. Pierce, Sherborne Press, 1970.
Mysteries of Egypt, L. Spence, Rider, 1929.
Myth and Symbol in Ancient Egypt, T. Rundle Clark, Thames & Hudson, 1959.
Practical Egyptian Magic, M. Hope, Aquarian Press, 1984.
The Way of Five Bodies, R. Masters, Amity, 1988.

Orphic
Pan and the Nightmare, J. Hillman and W. Rocher, Spring Books, 1972.
The Greek Myths, R. Graves (2 vols), Pelican, 1969.

The White Goddess, R. Graves, Faber & Faber, 1952.
The Metamorphoses, Ovid, Mentor Press, 1968.
Isis in the Graeco Roman World, R. Witt, Thames & Hudson, 1971.
Symbolism in Greek Mythology, P. Diel, Shambala, 1980.
The Gods of the Greeks, K. Kerenyi, Thames & Hudson, 1974.
Prolegomena, J. Harrison, Merlin Press, 1980.
Practical Greek Magic, M. Hope, Aquarian Press, 1985.

Celtic
The Flaming Door, E. Merry, Rider, 1936.
The Lost Gods of England, B. Branston, Thames & Hudson, 1974.
Glastonbury: Avalon of the Heart, D. Fortune, Aquarian Press, 1989.
Practical Celtic Magic, M. Hope, Aquarian Press, 1987.
Mysteries of Britain, L. Spence, Aquarian Press, 1979.
Glastonbury, A. Roberts, Rider, 1978.
Annals of the Sacred Isle, R.H. Caine, 1926.
The Western Way, J. and C. Matthews, Arkana, 1986.
The Celtic Tradition, C. Matthews, Element, 1989.

Navaho
The Book of the Navaho, R. Locke, Mankind Publications, 1976.
A Magic Dwells, S. Moon, Rider, 1972.
Navaho Witchcraft, C. Kluckthorn, Beacon Press, 1944.
On the Gleaming Way, J. Collier, Sage Press, 1962.
The Navaho, Kluckthorn and Leighton, Harvard University Press, 1974.

Slavonic
The Scythians, T. Talbot Rice, Thames & Hudson.
The Balts, M. Gimbutas, Thames & Hudson.

Workshops
Workshops on practical magic and all aspects of the Mysteries are organized by:
ARCANIA, 17 Union Passage, Bath, Avon, UK.
SOL, PO Box 215, St Helier, Jersey, Channel Isles, UK.
Kosmos, Prinzhendrikcade, Amsterdam, Holland.
De Pit, 166 Prinz Hendrik Straat, PT Breda, Holland.
Aledinck, Kerkstraat 26, 7722 LR Hoonhorst, Holland.
Isis Bookstore, 5701 E. Colfax Avenue, Denver, Colorado, USA.
SEED, 6000 Overbrook Avenue, Philadelphia, Pennsylvania, USA.
SOL America, PO Box 1146, Ann Arbor, Michigan, USA.

INDEX

Author's note:
Women interested in obtaining more information about the ritual of the reconsecration of the womb (see page 58) can contact the author through S.O.L., P.O. Box 215, St Helier, Jersey, Channel Islands, Great Britain, or through S.O.L. America, P.O. Box 1146, Ann Arbor, MI 48106, USA. Please include a stamped addressed envelope or, if writing to Jersey from overseas, a self-addressed envelope plus an International Reply Coupon.

By the same author . . .

THE SACRED CORD
MEDITATIONS

AN EVOLUTIONARY SPIRITUAL JOURNEY USING
THE ATLANTEAN ROSARY

The Sacred Cord or rosary has been used in almost every spiritual tradition as a basis for prayer or contemplation.

In this book Dolores Ashcroft-Nowicki tells how she first came to hear of the ancient Atlantean Sacred Cord and gives full instructions on how to make one, explaining the magical significance of each bead. She goes on to outline a meditational journey using the Cord, guiding the reader through the course of a year from the first bead, the birth of the untutored Primal Spark, to the last bead, the realization of divinity. Each set of beads brings greater insights into the self and awareness of the interrelationship between all living things on the Earth.

An important learning device for esoteric work and self-transformation, the Sacred Cord is a valuable aid to self-development, while the Sacred Cord meditation cycle presents a spiritual journey which is both uplifting and rewarding.

HIGHWAYS OF THE MIND

THE ART AND HISTORY OF PATHWORKING

Following the success of *The Shining Paths*, Dolores Ashcroft-Nowicki, the world's leading exponent of pathworking, here presents the definitive work on this ancient tradition.

Tracing them from the earliest cave paintings, through the Egyptian Book of the Dead, through the Bardic tradition and the storytellers of Ireland, she shows pathworkings to be part of a much greater structure in the make up of man, pertaining to his hopes and dreams, and his ability to make those dreams come true.

Used with purpose and by trained minds, the pathworking becomes a series of controlled thought patterns, and thought is the basis of creation.

INNER LANDSCAPES

A JOURNEY INTO AWARENESS BY PATHWORKING

Inner Landscapes outlines a series of guided meditation journeys, each using a Major Arcana Trump card from the beautiful *Servants of the Light Tarot*, and all linked by the central location of a stone circle which is reached by pathworking. After an introduction to the techniques and benefits of pathworking, the book guides the reader, chapter by chapter, card by card, into an integrated experience of the whole Major Arcana and a greater understanding of the Tarot. As each journey is completed, a figure from a Trump card takes form, so that by the end all the figures from the cards have materialized and the meaning of the cycle becomes clear.

Ultimately, these pathworkings can be adopted as a yearly or two-yearly discipline, bringing deepened insights as each cycle is completed. Through these guided meditational journeys the Tarot reader can extend psychic abilities, create a tranquil, secure retreat from outside stress, enhance understanding of Tarot symbolism, integrate new realizations into the whole of esoteric work.